# PRAISE FOR *SECURELY ATTACHED*

"*Securely Attached* is a resource that every therapist, client, and person needs in their life. Eli hands us her clear knowledge of the attachment research in a way that is engaging, concise, and hopeful toward healing attachment wounds and learning how to cultivate secure bonds with the people who matter most in our lives."

—DR. NICOLE LEPERA, @the.holistic.psychologist and *New York Times*–bestselling author of *How to Do the Work*

"Transforming our attachment patterns is a transformative journey, and Eli Harwood's book, *Securely Attached*, is a guiding light on this path of self-discovery and growth. With a blend of expertise, compassion, and personal experience, Eli empowers adults with insecure attachment styles to forge deeply satisfying and secure relationships."

—JESSICA BAUM, LMHC, author of *Anxiously Attached: Becoming More Secure in Life and Love*

"This visually engaging, humor-infused workbook guides insecurely attached readers on a journey of self-discovery. Harwood gently provides clear explanations of attachment-related concepts readers can apply to their lives through thought-provoking exercises. The result is an amazing opportunity to nurture secure attachment and enjoy emotionally intimate relationships."

—LESLIE BECKER-PHELPS, PHD, author of *Insecure in Love* and *Insecure in Love Workbook: Step-by-Step Guidance to Help You Overcome Anxious Attachment and Feel More Secure with Yourself and Your Partner*

"An important, user-friendly guide to understanding and transforming attachment patterns."

—L. ALAN SROUFE, professor emeritus, University of Minnesota

"You have decided to embark on a worthy and challenging endeavor by engaging this book. You're in good hands! Eli is going to give you the brainy stuff of how early relationships create patterns in our lives. And who is Eli? Perhaps you have watched one of her TikTok videos, or read her Instagram posts. This I can promise you: she is not just an academic or clinical expert worthy of a follow on social media. She is your ally. She has lived what she has written in this book, and she is cheering you on."

—ABBY WONG-HEFFTER, LMHC, trauma and abuse th

# Securely Attached

Transform Your
Attachment
Patterns into
Loving, Lasting
Romantic
Relationships

Eli
Harwood

 SASQUATCH BOOKS | SEATTLE

Dedicated to the love of my life.
Thank you for being the place where I am
seen, heard, loved, and challenged to grow.
I adore you.

# Contents

# Foreword

If you're cracking open this book, you're about to do something incredibly brave and wise. Brave, because looking (really looking) at your relationships is hard work—it means facing the painful patterns we learned growing up, the strategies we used to stay safe and close to imperfect people. And wise because more than 50 years of evidence shows just how incredibly valuable our relationships can be. What that evidence reveals is that forming close relationships is not simply a nice "extracurricular"—it's a core part of what makes us human. (More bluntly, when we're deprived of close relationships, our brains and bodies simply don't function well.) Doing the work to make those relationships more secure is a long-term investment in your mental health, romantic and sexual satisfaction, and physical wellness (even how long you live!). If you have kids—now or in the future—you're investing in their healthy development too.

As a relationship scientist, I've been conducting research on attachment for the past 10 years (and it's the coolest thing I can imagine doing). Every year, I teach college courses, write articles, and give lectures about how attachment shapes human development, and how to help our children, partners, clients, and ourselves become securely attached. It's a beautiful thing to watch people learn about attachment for the first time—it's like they've put on a pair of glasses that clarifies their past and present. My mentor, Dr. Jude Cassidy, calls this giving people "eyes to see" the world of relationships. What my students often say is, "I wish I knew about this sooner," or "I wish my parents had known about this when I was growing up."

But as much as I adore attachment and believe in its transformative power, doing this work has revealed what I see as two key limitations: First, attachment theory is notoriously hard to understand—its simple and elegant insights are often hidden behind long (painfully dry) academic texts, jargon, and paywalls. That's why what Eli has done in this book is so valuable. When you've got an "attachment nerd" like her in your corner, you can be confident you're getting the truth of what attachment theory actually says, what the research really shows, about building secure relationships. (Spoiler alert: you don't have to be a perfect parent, breastfeed endlessly, or be available 24/7 to raise a securely attached child.) But more importantly, this book manages to take decades of high-quality, complex academic research and boil it down to its core wisdom in a way that's easy to understand, actionable, funny, and simply delightful.

Before you cozy up with this book, however, it's important that you're aware of a second limitation: like many disciplines of psychology, studies of attachment have focused predominantly on white, cisgender, heterosexual people from Western, educated, industrialized, rich, and democratic (WEIRD) cultures. My colleagues and I are actively working on this issue, but the field has a long way to go to be more diverse, equitable, inclusive, and just. With those limitations in mind, here's what I believe the research does show:

1   Attachment—the capacity to form close relationships—is universal; therefore, everyone has a universal human right to create fulfilling relationships.

2   But the unique forms your attachment relationships take may look different depending on your culture, identities, and family structure, as well as the broader sociopolitical context (including systems of oppression like racism, classism, and homophobia). For example, if you grew up in a family of immigrants who faced the threat of deportation and family separation, your caregivers may have provided a secure base by keeping close tabs on your whereabouts or preparing you to deal with bias and xenophobia. If these behaviors helped you feel safe and connected, then they're an important part of your story and attachment security.

What I love about Eli's book is that it's for everybody. Some parts of the research may not resonate with your experience, and that's OK. I warmly invite you to bring your full self to this book, to lean into the joy and discomfort of exploring your attachment history, and to feel empowered to craft your attachment future with curiosity, compassion, and a healthy dose of science.

**JESSICA A. STERN, PhD**
Research Fellow
Department of Psychology, University of Virginia

# Before You Dig into This Attachment Journey

Welcome, friends! I am aware of the courage that it takes to do this work, and I am so glad you are here. The journey to finding and maintaining a deeply secure romantic relationship can feel extremely daunting, if not downright unattainable at times.

Why? Because within each of us lies an entire universe full of our childhoods and past relationship experiences and stories. When we become close to another person, our worlds collide. Building intimacy is beautiful and exciting and expands our world, but it can also trigger past pain and knee-jerk reactions that create distance and disconnection from our partners. This can lead to deeply unhappy relationships or to painful and costly breakups and divorces.

Trying to sort out how to get close to someone and stay close with someone can feel extremely challenging, especially if you are one of the 45 percent of people who grew up in a family who was unable to offer you a secure relationship experience.

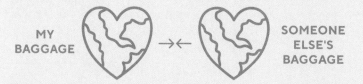

This book is what I wish I could have read in my twenties when I was scrambling all around town trying to figure out how to create a secure relationship with a partner. Unfortunately for me, there was no such book at the time, so I kept falling into the same potholes with different people and ending up on the same dead-end street. Instead of finding secure love, I found myself starting to worry that something was inherently flawed in me.

Eventually, I hired myself a shrink, or what my mom kindly refers to as a "rent-a-friend." It was in this therapy process that I learned all about attachment theory and it turned on all the lights upstairs for me. Learning about myself through an attachment lens, I started to believe that I wasn't unlovable. BUT that I did have some insecure patterns to work on. As I explored my attachment story, my emotional responses and behaviors in my romantic relationships made perfect sense.

I felt WAY less insecure and WAY more hopeful.

And guess what? It worked! I transformed an insecure pattern of relating into a secure pattern, and I took those skills and used them to build a deep, solid, and passionate relationship with the incredible human who is now my spouse.

I then went to graduate school in 2005 and after I completed my studies, I started a therapy practice where I have been nerding out on the magic of attachment research and its clinical applications with my incredible clients ever since.

And the biggest truth nugget I have found both in the science and in my clinic is this:

What happens in our lives as little people plays a big role in how we relate to our close friends and partners as adults.

When I share this message, I am aware that you might immediately imagine me as some odd HBO therapist stereotype wearing a paisley scarf and staring into the camera saying something painfully weird like "your inner child is handing you a zucchini, what do you think that means?" So let me just go ahead and reassure you that paisley is not my thing. Oh, and, changing your attachment strategy does not mean that you will be stuck in some creepy version of your past; in fact, it will help you do the opposite. By really doing the work to understand your attachment story, you will be able to shed some of the pain from it and move forward into the kind of connection you want now and in the future.

While all attachment strategies make sense in your childhood contexts, they don't all work to your advantage in creating the love you want now. Many of you will discover through this book that you had an insecure attachment experience and developed some insecure strategies to cope with that. I want to be clear up front: these insecure patterns are not personal defects. They are survival tools you used in your past relationships; they need to be transformed because they don't serve you in your quest to be securely attached.

If you find that you are one of the lucky half of people who has a secure strategy in attachment relationships, there is still lots of good reflection in here for you too. Some will be about your journey, and some may be about people you care for who haven't had the same secure experiences as you. This will still serve you as you continue to love people in an imperfect world!

# HOW TO USE THIS BOOK

I organized the book into three parts so you can get a sense of the three distinct tasks at hand in learning a secure attachment pattern.

**PART I** is about processing and grieving your childhood attachment experiences (yes, you are going to feel some feels). This is important because it helps you understand WHY you relate the way you do and WHAT it was that happened in your early relationships, which will allow your nervous system to release the pain from those experiences.

**PART II** is about how PART I got translated into your grown-up experiences. It is also about how your grown-up experiences either reinforced your insecure strategies, made them even more pronounced, or for the lucky ones, helped you move toward healing. If you have never had a serious romantic relationship, use this section to reflect on the ways you have navigated your closest friendships. Friends can absolutely be attachment figures for us.

**PART III** is about the tactical things you will need to learn and adapt now that you have processed your pain and original attachment stories. This section will break it down to the nitty gritty, so you have a solid idea of how to relate to others with a secure pattern.

**Look for the Key**
The book is also color-coded throughout to show you the distinctions between the four attachment categories in the different topics. Here's the key:

> **Green** = Secure
> **Yellow** = Ambivalent/Preoccupied
> **Blue** = Avoidant/Dismissive
> **Red** = Disorganized/Unresolved

**How long should I take to complete this?**
My invitation is to pace yourself. Healing is not a sprint. Give your mind and body time to catch up with the ideas you are learning and the work you are putting in to apply them to your life. Four to six pages a week is a great steady pace. If you are an Energizer Bunny and must go faster, I get it; I have the same problem. But take breaks if you start to feel overwhelmed or checked out. Your body might just need a minute to process what you are feeling and reflecting on.

# ATTACHMENT NERD ALERT

Y'all, I am a total nerd when it comes to attachment. And in my nerdiness I am a research-loyal gal. I don't feel good guiding people along a path if there isn't solid, observable, peer-reviewed evidence to support the likely outcomes. Just in case you all are a little bit nerdy too, I have summarized some of my favorite research facts and sprinkled them throughout in sections called "Attachment Nerd Alert."

# ATTACHMENT: MYTH OR FACT?

| MYTH | | FACT |
|------|---|------|
| "Attachment" means babies who are breastfed for a long time or sleep in their parent's bed and are raised with "attachment parenting." |  | The research is clear that the key to a secure attachment is an emotionally attuned caregiver, not how you ate or where you slept as a baby. |
| There is a category called "anxious attachment." |  | There are two attachment styles in the research categories that use the word "anxious" as a part of their names: <br> Anxious-ambivalent <br> Anxious-avoidant |
| What happens to you in the first few years of life is the attachment you develop forever. |  | While the first few years of life are very impactful to your attachment, you can experience significant shifts in your attachment throughout your life span. |
| You only have one attachment category. |  | This is not correlated with the bulk of attachment research. Because we are creatures who have more than one attachment relationship, it is possible we develop multiple strategies. |

| MYTH | | FACT |
|------|---|------|
| Your category is called your attachment "style." | 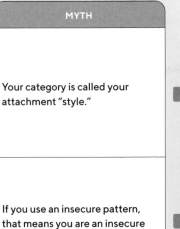 | This is a bit tricky. There is a set of research that uses this verbiage from social psychology, but it does not correlate with the developmental research. |
| If you use an insecure pattern, that means you are an insecure person. | | Nope. The word "insecure" is about the relational environment you grew up in, and then the corresponding strategy you had to develop in response. You are not insecure; your attachment relationships were. |
| "Avoidant attachment" means that someone is avoiding close relationships and does not want to be attached. | | Nope. Avoidance is a strategy designed to keep caregivers close without burdening them with emotional needs. Avoidant attachment avoids expressing distress and reaching to others, not attachment itself. |
| You can only be attached to parents or a romantic partner. | | Nope! You can form an attachment bond with anyone in your life, including friends. |

 **ATTACHMENT NERD ALERT**

Because I trust the developmental research the most (it is the data underlying this book), I will use the following terms throughout: "attachment pattern," "attachment category," and "attachment strategy," but not "attachment style."

**PART 1:**

# Where
# Your
# Story
# Began

_____

The real voyage of
discovery consists, not in
seeking new landscapes,
but in having new eyes.

**—MARCEL PROUST,**
*LA PRISONNIÈRE*

This section is going to be a deep dive into your early attachment experiences with the people who raised you. The goal is to help you understand WHY you think and act in relationships in very specific ways.

The most important rule in completing this section is to be as kind to yourself as you can-whether thinking in kindness terms in relation to a story about yourself when you were young, or being kind to yourself about the way the past is triggering emotion in you now. Being gentle toward yourself is part of learning to be gentler in general and therefore, more secure with other people.

If you start this work and it overwhelms you, please offer yourself the kindness of finding a therapist to walk the process with you, ESPECIALLY if you have experienced abuse and trauma in your relationships. Having a witness can make all the difference.

## FIVE HOT TIPS TO CONSIDER BEFORE STARTING YOUR ATTACHMENT JOURNEY

1    Hire yourself a therapist or coach who is attachment informed (it will be noted on their website or their other listings). It won't hurt to have a guide with you taking note of your stories and your process and answering questions that will inevitably come up. If you already know you have a lot of big attachment trauma, I hope you will offer yourself this kindness and not try to white-knuckle this process in isolation. You can find therapists through your insurance, or by googling "therapists near me." If finances are a limitation, you can also google "low fee" or "no fee" counseling clinics near me.

2    Share with one to three trustworthy friends that you are embarking on this journey and may need encouragement or caring ears and arms as you process some potentially emotional material.

**3** Get yourself some cozy socks or a new blanket, cuddle up with your cat, dog, or Labord's chameleon, and treat yourself to that favorite cup o' tea or joe while you read and journal to send a strong message to your body that you are safe and capable of this work!

**4** If you're an overachiever, start a book club! Get a group of other overachievers to work through and share their process with you step by step so you can normalize your experiences and learn from each other!

**5** Remember that no matter what you discover about your attachment story in this process, you are worthy of connection and healing. We all are.

# WHAT IS ATTACHMENT THEORY?

No other species on Earth is born as completely helpless and dependent as the human infant. Elephants walk seconds after they break through their gigantic amniotic sacs, a newborn baboon can cling to its mother's hair while she swings wildly through the trees. And there is a lizard called the Labord's chameleon that NEVER EVEN MEETS ITS PARENTS!

Then there is the human newborn over here, like, "Oh yeah, well I can almost see eight inches in front of my face and grab ahold of someone's pinky finger!"

While this dependency trait might seem like a liability to our kind, it is actually the very thing that allows our brains to develop such complex gray matter in our prefrontal cortex. Our attachment drive is the advantage that sets human beings apart as the only (currently discovered) species with verbal capacity and the ability to mentalize and meta-process, which means that we can make meaning out of our experiences and learn from the experiences of others.

But of course, that doesn't mean that all parents are equally properly equipped to care for their children. The specifics of how our individual caregivers respond, especially in early childhood, become a thematic template for the way we relate to others, the way we feel about our feelings, and whether we can effectively utilize our social relationships to thrive.

If a human being is a computer, then the attachment instinct is the built-in hard drive; everyone has one. The way your caregivers handle your attachment needs is the software that gets installed on your hard drive. Not all software programs function the same way. Some software programs install secure-loving connection, some install disconnected-avoidance, some install intrusive or unpredictable ambivalence, and some have viruses and a mix of erratic disorganized responses.

In later research, through longitudinal studies on the Strange Situation, and through the Adult Attachment Interview research of Mary Main and Eric Hesse at the University of California, Berkeley, attachment scientists were able to prove the link between early childhood attachment patterns, as well as adulthood patterns. They were also able to categorize children who had been abused or severely neglected and how that shaped their adult minds.

| CHILDHOOD | ADULTHOOD |
|---|---|
| ◀ Insecure Anxious Ambivalent* | ◀ Preoccupied |
| ◀ Insecure Anxious Avoidant | ◀ Dismissive |
| ◀ Disorganized | ◀ Unresolved Disorganized |
| ◀ Secure | ◀ Secure Autonomous |

*Often mistakenly labeled only as "anxious"

There is a consensus in the research that people fall into one of four categories of attachment patterns. These four strategies are distinct coping responses based on the level of availability, consistency, safety, and effectiveness of caregiver responses.

Around half of people fall into the only category considered to be a "secure" attachment, cleverly titled "secure attachment style."

Everyone else falls into one of the three insecure categories (which annoyingly have different names in childhood than they do in adulthood. I have grouped them together throughout this book to avoid as much confusion as possible and help you connect them together as one style with two titles).

Though an insecure attachment experience does mean a harder path to finding secure love, it is not a lifelong suffering sentence. In fact, there is another category in the research termed an "earned secure attachment," for those of us who have had to put in our own work to learn secure relating skills.

Remember our computer analogy? Earning a secure attachment strategy is about rewriting the code in our software program. You can't simply delete the software, but you can eliminate any viruses and you can change the way it works and add new code to adjust its function.

So, let's workbook out whatever insecurity lies in your attachment strategy and rewrite the necessary skills into your code so you can join me over here in the land of earned security!

## ATTACHMENT NERD ALERT

Starting in the 1950s, researchers John Bowlby, Mary Ainsworth, and Harry Harlow pioneered the science behind attachment theory. They theorized that what happens in infancy between caregivers and babies has an impact on the mental and social development of children that affects a person's whole life trajectory.

Through Harlow's Monkey Love experiments and Ainsworth's Strange Situation experiment, it became clear that primate and human babies are significantly affected by the level of nurture they are given by their attachment figures (usually mothers).

Further research from Elizabeth Carlson and Alan Sroufe at the University of Minnesota (where I was trained to score the Strange Situation research tool), has continued this rich legacy of attachment study, looking at the impact attachment has on cortisol levels, addiction to opioids, the impact of foster care and divorce, and lifelong relationship to resilience.

## What attachment category best describes your pattern?

Select the answer below each question that best describes your experiences and instincts.

1    When you were upset or scared as a child, what do you remember doing to cope?

◀ Playing with my toys or distracting myself.

◀ Running to a caregiver but feeling mad and upset for a long time.

◀ Running to a caregiver and feeling soothed quickly.

◀ Feeling lost, stuck, scared, and sometimes full of rage.

2    What were the messages in your childhood home(s) about feelings?

◀ Your feelings matter and you can always get support when you need it.

◀ Mixed messages—sometimes it was OK to feel, sometimes it wasn't.

◀ Your feelings are selfish or mean or shameful.

◀ Don't focus on what you feel, try to be logical.

3    When you are upset or scared as a grown-up, what is your go-to response?

◀ Call my people frantically and freak out until I crash.

◀ Try not to think about it and move on.

◀ Go into destruct mode or completely shut down.

◀ Reach out to my people, share my feelings, and receive their care.

4    What is something that friends or romantic partners have said about how you respond to their pain?

◀ "I can never tell what you are feeling."

◀ "You always make it about you when it is not."

◀ "You always know how to make me feel better."

◀ "There is no one in the world who responds to me faster than you do."

**5** When someone offers you empathy when you are emotional, what happens in your body?

◀ I get uncomfortable and want to change the subject.

◀ I start overflowing with all the pain from all the things.

◀ I feel soothed and calmed.

◀ I question the person's motives and start feeling agitated or shut down.

**6** When someone you care about is crying, what is closest to your response?

◀ I do whatever I can to rescue them; their pain is my pain.

◀ I offer kindness and empathy.

◀ I tell them to suck it up, they don't know what real pain is.

◀ I give an awkward hug, or word of kindness and then make a quick exit.

**7** When something disappointing happens in a relationship of yours, what does your inner voice sound like?

◀ "Get over it, it's not a big deal, you'll be fine."

◀ "Why are they doing this to me? Do I not matter to them?"

◀ "I am sad and that is valid, but I will be okay."

◀ "You deserve this, you dumb dumb."

**8** When you imagine getting emotionally close to someone, what is your response?

◀ Hyper-excitement

◀ Discomfort

◀ Oscillating between fear and desperation

◀ Groundedness

**9** When someone trustworthy asks you about your childhood, what is your response?

 "My childhood? Let me tell you what my mom did just yesterday . . ."

 "There was no good. Just the bad and the ugly."

 "It was good. I don't really remember much, but good I think."

 "There were some hard things, but my family was always loving with me."

**10** What phrase best suits the way you would describe your emotional health?

 I'm fine. I don't really feel much.

 Stable overall.

 Sometimes I am numb, but mostly I struggle and feel disoriented.

 If my relationships are good, I am great. If not, I feel wretched.

**Total up the number of questions you circled in each color. The color with the most answers is your dominant attachment strategy. Read more about your strategy on the next spread.**

 _____

 _____

 _____

 _____

 Secure   Ambivalent/Preoccupied
 **Avoidant/Dismissive**   **Disorganized/Unresolved**

The capacity for self-soothing is born out of hundreds and hundreds of instances of being soothed by someone else.

—RACHEL SAMSON,
@AustralianPsychologist

# ATTACHMENT CATEGORIES

| SECURE ATTACHMENT | INSECURE PREOCCUPIED ATTACHMENT | INSECURE DISMISSIVE ATTACHMENT | INSECURE DISORGANIZED ATTACHMENT |
|---|---|---|---|
| **CHILDHOOD NAME** | | | |
| Secure | Anxious Ambivalent | Anxious Avoidant | Insecure Disorganized Attachment |
| **ADULTHOOD NAME** | | | |
| Secure or Autonomous | Preoccupied | Dismissive Avoidant | Fearful Attachment |
| **INFANT ATTACHMENT CHARACTERISTICS** | | | |
| • Cries when in distress<br>• Seeks proximity to caregivers when distressed<br>• Maintains proximity to caregivers<br>• Is easily reassured and calmed | • Cries when in distress<br>• Actively seeks proximity to caregivers<br>• Protests upon reunion/Does not maintain contact<br>• Does not soothe easily | • Does not outwardly express distress<br>• Does not seek caregiver upon reunion<br>• Does not maintain closeness to caregiver<br>• Looks calm outwardly, but has high cortisol | • Erratic behavior when distressed<br>• Oscillates between fight, flight, and freeze<br>• Appears afraid of caregiver<br>• Is not calmed in proximity of caregiver |
| **ADULT RELATIONSHIP TENDENCIES** | | | |
| • Loving and supportive when others are emotional<br>• Seeks support when upset<br>• Communicates needs verbally and directly<br>• Easily soothed through empathy | • Hypervigilant about others' feelings<br>• Needs frequent reassurance<br>• Communicates needs dramatically<br>• Does not feel easily reassured or soothed | • Uncomfortable in the presence of emotions<br>• Seeks distraction when upset<br>• Does not communicate emotional needs to others<br>• Finds empathy and nurture uncomfortable | • Oscillates between clinging and pushing<br>• Feels angry and disoriented when emotional<br>• Struggles to trust the intentions of anyone<br>• Does not feel safe in any attachment relationship |
| **PRIMARY COPING** | | | |
| Connection | Hypervigilance | Distraction | Defensiveness and Mistrust |
| **NERVOUS SYSTEM INCLINATIONS** | | | |
| Regulated Pattern (Reach and Relief) | Hyperarousal (Reach and Reject and Repeat) | Hypoarousal (Avoid and Retreat) | Fight/Flight/Freeze (Battle, Flee, or Dissociate) |

## Earned Secure Attachment

WAIT! There's one more category . . .

And it's the entire reason I wrote this book (and likely one of the reasons you bought it).

It's called EARNED Secure Attachment.

Which means this: A person grows up in a home that is insecure, and they inherit that pattern of attachment as a result. But then (drum roll please), they grow up and realize it's not working to get them the secure love that they want.

SO, THEY (YOU!!!) WORK THEIR TUCHES OFF AND HEAL AND GROW.

How cool is that?

The answer is very, very cool.

# PEOPLE DO NOT BELONG IN BOXES

The goal in this process is not to give yourself a strict label or start to see all people as limited to one color/strategy of attachment. No one IS an attachment pattern; instead, see these categories as illuminating what you went through in the past and the coping strategies you used as a result.

It is not uncommon, in fact, to find yourself relating to more than one category. That is because these strategies develop in relationships. For example, if you had more than one caregiver, and each one had a unique pattern with you, then you would have to adapt accordingly.

I had a different attachment strategy to my mom than to my dad. Then add in all the other people I developed close relationships with as I grew. Lots of different experiences there, so lots of variance in my strategies in relationships. Plus, friends can be attachment figures for us.

AND, when you date people, the intensity of their strategy might evoke a different expression of your strategy. My primary strategy was ambivalent/preoccupied, but I once dated someone more intense in that same category and it activated a more avoidant/dismissive response from me.

As you work through this journey, the goal is to learn to recognize and acknowledge any pieces of ◀ red (disorganized), ◀ yellow (preoccupied), and ◀ blue (dismissive) strategies that you have acquired either in childhood or through traumatic adult relationships, and work to transform those strategies to ◀ greener (secure) pastures!

# ATTACHMENT ACROSS DEVELOPMENTAL STAGES

### In Utero
YES! Babies are LITERALLY attached to their birth mother/parent. In utero, babies need their caregivers to take good care of their bodies and follow as many medical recommendations for pregnancy as possible. They also need their caregiver to start bonding with them through cooing, singing, and seeing them as belonging together.

### Birth through Infancy
Babies need high levels of proximity (closeness to caregivers) and high responsiveness from those caregivers when they communicate either by crying or cooing. They are learning that their cries bring support (or that there is no point in crying out).

### Toddlerhood
These littles need lots of support with their big feelings to learn what is happening in their body and how to cope with it. They also need safe, reasonable limits from caregivers to learn about safe/appropriate and unsafe/inappropriate choices.

### Preschool Age
Preschoolers need lots of presence and engagement with their excitement for the world. They continue to have big rushes of emotions so need compassionate understanding and guidance from attachment figures and good examples of coping skills.

### School Age

School-age kids are learning about relationships and the world at rapid rates, so they need lots of time to ask questions and explore ideas. They also need continued emotional understanding and education about their feelings and needs as their relationships grow in complexity.

### Early Adolescence (Tweens)

Tweens are in the middle of huge physiological changes that affect the way they see their bodies and their peers. They need honest education about those changes that help protect them from shame and misinformation. They need patience and playfulness as they enter a stage of life that can feel scary and overwhelming.

### Adolescence (Teenagers)

Teenagers are practice adults. They are learning how to be independent and to take responsibility for their own decisions. They need their attachment figures to give them space to make their own choices, while simultaneously being a secure base for support and understanding. Teenagers need parents to give them ongoing love and encouragement but also to hand them the baton with increasing frequency so they can grow.

### Adulthood

We tend to transfer our attachment needs from our parents to our peers, and most intensely to our romantic partners. Here we seek belonging, connection, comfort, and support in these relationships outside of our families of origin.

## Who were your early attachment figures?

Your primary attachment figures are the people who were most frequently in charge of your care when you were small. They changed your diapers (I hope!), AND they responded (or didn't) to your cries and coos. Use these prompts to help you come up with adjectives associated with your early attachment figures, which we'll then use to sort into categories.

---

Who were the one to two parent figures in your life that primarily took care of you as a child? (If you had severe attachment trauma and ended up in temporary care settings like foster care, you may have a longer list here.) Add as many primary caregivers to the list as you had in your life.

1 _____

2 _____

_____

_____

_____

When you think about the people who cared for you in your younger years (0–5), what are three to five words you would use to describe the way your relationship with them made you feel? (Use the chart on page 18 as a guide if you are struggling to find words.)

3 to 5 Words: Caregiver 1

1 _____

2 _____

3 _____

4 _____

5 _____


3 to 5 Words: Caregiver 2

1 _____

2 _____

3 _____

4 _____

5 _____

Write a couple of sentences for each caregiver that describe their philosophy of taking care of you. Did it change as you aged? Did it stay consistent or loop de loop all over the place?

Caregiver 1

Caregiver 2

Circle or fill in adjectives about your caregivers that came up frequently on the previous page to match the categories most accurately below. It's OK to have adjectives across all or most categories!

| SECURE CAREGIVERS | Warm | _____ |
| | Empathetic | _____ |
| | Connected | _____ |
| | _____ | _____ |
| | _____ | _____ |
| | _____ | _____ |
| | _____ | _____ |

| AMBIVALENT CAREGIVERS | Anxious | _____ |
| | Intrusive | _____ |
| | Overwhelming | _____ |
| | _____ | _____ |
| | _____ | _____ |
| | _____ | _____ |
| | _____ | _____ |

|                          | Logic-focused | _____ |
|                          | Practical     | _____ |
|                          | Stoic         | _____ |
| **DISMISSIVE CAREGIVERS** | _____ | _____ |
|                          | _____ | _____ |
|                          | _____ | _____ |
|                          | _____ | _____ |

|                          | Scary      | _____ |
|                          | Neglectful | _____ |
|                          | Erratic    | _____ |
| **FEARFUL CAREGIVERS**   | _____ | _____ |
|                          | _____ | _____ |
|                          | _____ | _____ |
|                          | _____ | _____ |

### What attachment strategy did your caregivers use with you?

Attachment is not genetic or personality-based, but rather a response to the ways that our caregivers relate to us, especially in times of tender need and distress.

In other words, when you were emotional or needing closeness, what reaction did your primary attachment figures have to your needs? That response, for better or for worse, created a response (coping skill) in you.

---

Place check marks next to the qualities that resonate with your experience with your caregivers. If you're doing this exercise for more than one attachment figure, use different symbols to differentiate them.

| SECURE CAREGIVERS | DISMISSIVE CAREGIVERS |
|---|---|
| ☐ Acknowledge and validate child's feelings | ☐ Dismiss/ignore/intellectualize child's feelings |
| ☐ Act as a secure base when kids are scared, sad, ashamed, angry, or dysregulated | ☐ Focus on making kids "independent" instead of comforting them and being a place of refuge |
| ☐ Have a warm demeanor | ☐ Tend to feel distant or disconnected |
| ☐ Can talk about hard things calmly | ☐ Avoid topics that are emotional |
| ☐ Say sorry when they mess up | ☐ Get more distant when they mess up |
| ☐ Initiate repair when there is conflict | ☐ Avoid conflict or "move on" |

| PREOCCUPIED CAREGIVERS | DISORGANIZED CAREGIVERS |
|---|---|
| ☐ Overreact to child's feelings | ☐ React scarily to child's feelings |
| ☐ Intrude their emotional responses onto their child's pain | ☐ Punish their children for their needs or emotional reactions |
| ☐ Have an anxious demeanor | ☐ Have an unpredictable personality and feel scary to a child frequently |
| ☐ Get spun up in emotional conversations | ☐ Misread the intentions of others in heated conversations |
| ☐ Fixate on conflict and sometimes can't let things go either something they did or something a kid did | ☐ Are constantly triggering conflict and accusing children of malintent |

## Affection and connection

Physical affection (hugs, kisses, snuggles, etc.), helps kids feel belonging and security. It fills their hearts with a story like, "I am loved, I matter, I can rely on people." When there is an absence in this area, it leaves a hole that kids usually fill with a story like: "I am unworthy or not good enough or don't matter." (Kids with sensory processing issues may not like physical affection as much, but they still need other forms of affection, like words and acts of service.)

Did you receive hugs or physical holding as a child? Did that touch feel natural and soothing, or did it feel uncomfortable and forced?

Did your caregivers use loving words to express their adoration to you? Did their words feel genuine or perfunctory (it felt like they said it because they were supposed to)? Or did loving words feel conditional (they only said loving things when you did things that pleased them)?

What did you wish for as a child in terms of affection? If you could go back to your younger self as an adult, what would you say to them? How would you respond to your needs for affection?

How do you think the pattern of affection (or lack thereof) has affected how you currently give and receive physical and emotional affection in your close relationships as an adult?

# LOOKING IN

There is a very important term in attachment study called "attunement." It describes the process of one person using the external cues (facial expression, tone of voice, body movement, pace of speech, eye contact or lack thereof, etc.) to try to "read" the internal state another person is experiencing.

When someone reads our internal world as a child, it helps validate our existence, our needs, and our connectedness to others.

Children rely on parents to be emotionally attuned for three very important developmental tasks:

1   To be able to identify their emotional states and put language to them.

2   To be able to understand their emotional states and how to cope with them in socially effective ways.

3   To feel safe showing emotions to others and getting comfort when needed.

4   If your parents were skilled with attunement, then you likely have a good awareness of what you feel, and a kind narrative toward yourself when you feel it.

If your parents struggled to accurately read your internal state you might struggle to believe your feelings are valid, or think you are to blame for what you are feeling, and so on. You may also struggle to read the emotions of others with accuracy.

### Attunement and mis-attunement in your body

Think of a time that a caregiver accurately read your internal state and could tell you were feeling sad, scared, ashamed, angry, joyful, etc. What did that feel like for you? How did that affect the way you felt and what you thought about what you were feeling?

_____

_____

_____

_____

_____

_____

_____

_____

_____

_____

Now think of a time that a caregiver inaccurately read your internal state. Either they never noticed, or they inaccurately read your emotional state. What did that feel like for you? How did that affect the way you felt and what you thought about what you were feeling?

_____

_____

_____

_____

_____

_____

_____

_____

_____

_____

## ATTACHMENT NERD ALERT

Did you know that babies as young as 12 months of age already have an idea of whether their caregivers are capable of handling their emotional needs?

The data from Mary Ainsworth's Strange Situation research protocol reveals that what happens in our early experiences shapes a pattern of relating for us, even in a period of development that we cannot cognitively remember.

**The research experiment goes like this:**

1   A caregiver and a baby 12 to 18 months old are put into a room with toys and a stranger.

2   After a few minutes, the caregiver leaves the baby alone with the stranger.

3   Then after three minutes, the caregiver returns for a reunion.

4   Then the stranger leaves the room, and the caregiver and the baby are left alone for a few minutes.

5   Then the caregiver leaves the baby alone in the room for another three minutes.

6   Then the caregiver returns for a second reunion.

7   This experiment is designed to activate a child's distress levels to observe the way they use their caregiver as a source of comfort and support (or not).

Here are the four patterns that are scored in this research protocol:

**SECURE ATTACHMENT** Some babies know that their caregivers will be there for them and so cry upon separation (they don't want them to leave!). They then seek and reach for them upon reunion, where they are then easily soothed (within three minutes).

**AVOIDANT ATTACHMENT** Some babies already know that their caregivers cannot help them with their emotional needs. They feel stress in their bodies upon separation but do not express it outwardly and do not reach for their caregivers at the reunions.

**AMBIVALENT ATTACHMENT** Some babies know that their caregivers are unpredictable with their needs, sometimes helpful, sometimes not. They cry when they leave, and they seek them upon reunion, but they do not soothe upon reunion and protest and show anger at their caregiver.

**DISORGANIZED ATTACHMENT** Some babies have caregivers who are abusive or neglectful. Their responses to distress do not have a coherent pattern. Their attachment system is confused because their caregivers are often the cause of their distress.

This research tool helped solidify the categories of attachment. It has been replicated internationally and across various countries and has been linked to longitudinal data (which means the babies are studied and tracked across their lifetime).

Secure babies fare better across their development in physical, emotional, and social domains both in later childhood and in adulthood.

## The cost of separation and loss

Not everyone has the privilege of consistent proximity to their care-givers, and many people experience a complete loss of caregiv-ers. The impact of long-term separation or permanent loss is big. Whether you lost time with a caregiver because of divorce or death, incarceration, a relinquishment and ensuing adoption or foster expe-rience, or a reason you have yet to uncover, it creates a wound in your attachment system.

If you did have a prolonged separation with your attachment figures, what do you know about how old you were when it happened? How long was the separation? How did you cope with it?

What narratives were given to you about that separation or loss? Were you told you were lucky or that you were better off? Were you given permission to be sad and confused?

Did anyone nurture your heart during this time? If not, what did you do to cope with your grief?

_____

_____

_____

_____

_____

_____

_____

_____

Have you been given (or made) space to process any grief around this part of your attachment story? How do you think this loss has affected the way you interact in close relationships?

_____

_____

_____

_____

_____

_____

_____

_____

_____

_____

_____

_____

_____

**SECURE TIP**

When we acknowledge the sad things that have happened to us with caring witnesses, it helps us to reduce feelings of guilt and shame that cloud our healing process.

## Pictures of emotional closeness

Using stick figures and symbols below, draw a picture that represents your childhood relationship to your one or two most primary attachment figures. Think about how emotionally close or distant you felt from them and incorporate that space into the drawing. Think about how your body reacted in their presence as a child. Think about how their body appeared. If there are different settings that change the dynamic, draw a few scenes. (For example: holidays, sports settings, day vs. night, etc.)

### Trauma and attachment: What obstacles did your attachment figures face?

Secure attachment is a human instinct, but it can be throttled because of context and circumstances. Racial trauma, systemic oppression, financial burdens, war, mental illness, immigration trauma, substance abuse disorders, religious traumas, and the like can all get in the way of parents being able to offer children a warm, secure style of relating.

What do you know about the obstacles that your parents were facing in their lives that may have impaired their ability to be emotionally nurturing or caring with you?

What role has oppression played in your family history? Do you think that your parents may have learned trauma-based parenting strategies because of ancestral trauma? (For example, my father's maternal great-grandparents disappeared in Russia during the Bolshevik revolution, and his grandparents immigrated to the United States in duress during that time. As a result, their parent-child relationship was secondary to survival and was far more control-based than connection-based.)

How do you think your parents were parented? Do you think they did things differently with you than their parents did with them?
*If you have parents, grandparents, aunts, or uncles, or similar figures who are accessible and open to it, you can ask them if they have thoughts on any of these questions.*

# WHEN YOUR CAREGIVER'S BEHAVIOR CREATES TRAUMA

Remember how I shared earlier that our attachment drive helps keep us safe from predators we would otherwise have no chance to survive? You can visualize the creeping tiger and an attachment figure grabbing their baby and running to a shelter to escape. Attachment success!!

But what happens when the parent IS ALSO a predator with you? Yeah, it's not good. Abuse, neglect, and trauma from a caregiver deeply f*ck with your attachment pattern and lead to a disorganized and disorienting experience.

Running from a tiger (danger) into the arms of a grizzly bear (a dangerous parent) doesn't feel comforting. So, the nervous system tends to go into hyper-drive (freak out and act out), or hypo-drive (freeze and dissociate).

To make it even more complex, abusive, mentally ill, or addicted parents aren't always out of control; they sometimes act calm. So a child is not only faced with a parent who acts in scary ways, they are also left to try to predict when the next bad turn is coming. And in the case of abuse, they are often told that the abusive treatment is their fault (they are being "disciplined").

**REPEAT AFTER ME:**
No child is ever responsible for the way an adult behaves, acts, or thinks.

**Lions and tigers and bears, oh my**

Did you ever feel scared of one of your early caregivers?

Was there anyone there to stand up for you or protect you?

_____

_____

_____

_____

_____

_____

_____

_____

_____

_____

_____

_____

_____

_____

_____

_____

_____

_____

_____

_____

_____

_____

_____

_____

_____

_____

_____

_____

When the abuse or neglect was happening, who did you think was to blame for the frightening behavior your caregiver exhibited?

_____

_____

_____

_____

_____

_____

_____

_____

_____

_____

_____

_____

_____

_____

_____

_____

_____

_____

_____

_____

_____

_____

_____

_____

_____

_____

_____

_____

_____

_____

If you could visit that scene now as a grown-up and help your younger self, what would you do to provide care and support?

_____

_____

_____

_____

_____

_____

_____

_____

_____

_____

_____

_____

_____

_____

_____

_____

_____

_____

**SECURE TIP**

The two things that must be done to heal from childhood abuse, are (1) processing the pain from that trauma in the presence of a caring person so you can truly understand what it was you went through, and (2) transforming your perspective on your younger self, removing the shame you gained from the trauma, and replacing it with a view of compassion, love, and even pride for how you survived their mistreatment.

# DID YOU INHERIT GENERATIONAL TRAUMA?

"Generational trauma" is a phrase we use to describe what happens when the really bad and awful things that happen in one generation never get resolved or acknowledged or healed, so instead, they are passed down to the next generation.

No one tells you that they are offloading you with some painful energy and traumatic junk. Instead, you inherit generational trauma through:

1   The patterns your family uses to deal with pain, like:
    ◀ Avoiding talking about emotional pain.
    ◀ Punishing children for crying or being scared.
    ◀ Helicoptering or hovering with big anxiety over children.

2   The ways your family tells stories (or NOT!), like:
    ◀ Inappropriately scary and traumatizing unresolved storytelling.
    ◀ An absence of storytelling in general about the past.
    ◀ Obsessive talking about unresolved things without any hope.

3   The belief systems that your family has about suffering, like:
    ◀ Pain is meant to be handled alone.
    ◀ All pain is a crisis and is handled with intense anxiety.
    ◀ It is your fault if you are in pain.

4   Your genes. No joke. These can happen in any of the insecure categories:
    ◀ High occurrences of mental illness in your family tree
    ◀ High occurrences of substance abuse/addiction in your family tree
    ◀ High occurrences of divorce or family splits in your family tree

---

◀ Secure   ◀ Ambivalent/Preoccupied
◀ **Avoidant/Dismissive**   ◀ **Disorganized/Unresolved**

---

Google "epigenetics and trauma" if you want to nerd out!

## Archaeological dig activity

If you have family members that you trust enough to ask questions, this activity is meant to help you learn as much as you can about your family history.

Tell them you are working on how to have healthy, loving relationships and ask them if they could tell you anything they know about your family history. Were there any sudden deaths in your family? Illnesses? Family secrets? Cultural traumas? Use the space below to write out the information they share with you.

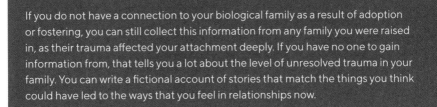

If you do not have a connection to your biological family as a result of adoption or fostering, you can still collect this information from any family you were raised in, as their trauma affected your attachment deeply. If you have no one to gain information from, that tells you a lot about the level of unresolved trauma in your family. You can write a fictional account of stories that match the things you think could have led to the ways that you feel in relationships now.

## Cultural identity inventory

The groups we belong to influence how we view ourselves and our relationships. How parents respond to attachment needs can be influenced by culture. Fill out these identity questions to prepare you for the next reflection.

What is your ethnic background? (e.g., Nigerian, Irish, Inuit, Bangladeshi, etc.)

What is your racial identity? (e.g., Black, Asian, Middle Eastern, White, Biracial, etc.)

What is your country or national identity? (If you have lived in many places, they all count!)

What religious communities did you grow up in? (Growing up non-religious is its own religious identity too!)

What socioeconomic world did you grow up in? (I grew up middle class, as evidenced by my enduring need to tell everyone what a deal I got on something.)

## Culture and attachment

Every unique culture has a differing perspective on the caregiver-child relationship. National, ethnic, racial, socioeconomic, and religious cultures bring different belief systems and traditions that impact how a parent and child interact.

What cultural beliefs about the parent–child dynamic do you think were present in your family system while you were developing and growing up? For what reasons do you think these beliefs and traditions were adopted into your culture?

_____

_____

_____

_____

_____

_____

_____

_____

_____

_____

Which of these beliefs, both positive and negative, do you think has had the biggest impact on your emotional world?

_____

_____

_____

_____

_____

_____

_____

_____

_____

Which of these cultural attitudes do you want to take with you and keep?

_____

_____

_____

_____

_____

_____

_____

_____

_____

_____

_____

_____

_____

_____

Which of these cultural attitudes do you want to edit or even relinquish?

_____

_____

_____

_____

_____

_____

_____

_____

_____

_____

_____

_____

_____

_____

# TENDER NEEDS AND DISTRESS

Human beings are emotional creatures. And our attachment drive is triggered by those emotional states. When we feel distressed, our body is wired to send us seeking our attachment people for help. Those people in turn give us meaning about our feelings and what we are supposed to do with them.

Here is a breakdown of the five big emotions and related questions to give you some insight into the various emotional states that may have been tender for you:

## The Big Five Emotions

### Joy

The experience of delight and satisfaction. What were the messages in your attachment relationships about joy? When you were in a state of joy, how did your caregivers respond to you?

### Sadness

The experience of loss. What were the messages in your attachment relationships about sadness? When you were in a state of sadness, how did your caregivers respond to you?

## Anger

The experience of feeling violated, neglected, or misunderstood. What were the messages in your attachment relationships about anger? When you were in a state of anger, how did your caregivers respond to you?

## Fear

The experience of feeling unsafe. What were the messages in your attachment relationships about fear? When you were in a state of fear, how did your caregivers respond to you?

## Shame

The experience of feeling unworthy. What were the messages in your attachment relationships about shame? When you were in a state of shame, how did your caregivers respond to you?

## Forbidden feelings

In most families, there is a scale of what emotions are more and less acceptable to caregivers. In families with insecure patterns, there is usually a pronounced emotion or two that are simply not allowed. All people feel sad, scared, angry, jealous, and embarrassed, but, unfortunately, not all caregivers make space for that.

In your childhood, what emotions were considered problematic and "not allowed" in your home?

_____

_____

_____

_____

_____

_____

_____

_____

_____

How did your caregivers respond when you had those feelings? What did they say or do?

_____

_____

_____

_____

_____

_____

_____

_____

_____

_____

_____

Why do you think your caregivers treated these specific feelings the way they did?

_____

_____

_____

_____

_____

_____

_____

_____

_____

Imagine that you had been allowed to feel those feelings freely as a child. How do you think that would have impacted you? What events in your childhood triggered those "forbidden feelings"? What did you need your caregivers to understand about what you were going through?

_____

_____

_____

_____

_____

_____

_____

_____

_____

**SECURE TIP**

In our close relationships, our partners and friends need us to offer acceptance of what they feel, even if those feelings make us nervous or uncomfortable. When we are receptive to what our partners and friends feel, then they no longer feel alone in their emotions. This is soothing and helps both people regulate.

## Secrets: Hidden traumas

When children go through painful and traumatic things and do not feel safe or comfortable sharing them with their attachment figures, it not only prevents healing of those traumas, but it also compounds feeling isolated and in deep pain.

Were there painful or important experiences in your childhood that you concealed from your caregivers? (This is common with sexual abuse, as children often don't have the language to even express what they experienced and are afraid it will reflect shamefully on them.)

What did you fear would happen if they found out?

Have you attended to these traumas later in life with friends or a partner or a therapist?

_____

_____

_____

_____

_____

_____

_____

_____


If you were to give this younger part of yourself exactly what they needed, what would you do or say or how would you help?

_____

_____

_____

_____

_____

_____

_____

_____

_____

_____

_____

_____

_____

_____

_____

_____

# WHAT IN THE GENDER?

Quick definitions for you:

**Medical sex**

Your medical *sex* is determined by your chromosomes and the genitalia you develop as a result. Male, female, or intersex are the medical sex categories that can be put in your medical file at birth. (Fun fact for you: there are more than XX (male) and XY (female) chromosome sets in human nature; there are 13 different known combinations and some complex private-part formations that happen in response to those chromosome sets!)

**Gender**

Your *gender* is what the culture then expects of you based on your determined sex.

If you were gendered as a boy at birth, research says you may have been cuddled less because you were already expected to be tough, despite barely seeing two inches in front of your face.

If you were gendered as a girl at birth, you are often socialized early on in childhood that your role is to take care of and please others, even when you can't yet wipe your own bottom.

**Cultural expectations**

Gender expectations evolve throughout your development (and throughout human history!), differ across cultures, and can be a major thing (or not) in your story.

This is important when we think about our childhood attachment experiences, because the ways our caregivers thought about gender affected the ways they responded to our emotional needs. Families with more strict gender ideas ("Women belong in the kitchen!" "Men must be tough!"), are going to create more insecure attachment patterns because of condemning natural emotional states. ("Boys don't cry." "Angry girls are b*tchy.")

## Attachment and your gender role

How do you think your childhood gender roles and expectations affected your relationships with your caregivers? Which caregiver were you close to or felt understood you?

What behaviors or preferences did your caregivers see as "off limits" for you because of your gender?

Did your gender affect your feelings of self-worth?

_____
_____
_____
_____
_____
_____
_____
_____
_____
_____
_____
_____
_____
_____
_____

Are there any expressions of yourself that you would like to reclaim as yours, despite not being a part of your family's expectations of your gender?

_____
_____
_____
_____
_____
_____
_____
_____
_____
_____
_____
_____
_____
_____

## ⌐◠-◠ ATTACHMENT
## ♥ NERD ALERT

Did you know that your body's chemistry is affected by the way people relate to you?

For example: If someone gives you a hug (that you wanted), your brain releases oxytocin. If someone aggressively yells at you, your body releases norepinephrine.

These chemicals not only affect how you physically feel in an emotional moment, but they also affect the way your brain functions over time. Children who receive lots of love and affection and care from their early caregivers develop brains that are accustomed to being soothed (i.e., thicker neocortex development). Children who have lots of chaos or danger in their early relationships tend to have brains that are accustomed to alertness and anxiety or dissociation and depression (i.e., larger amygdala).

And putting effort in to do healing work (like you are right now!!!) also changes the brain. Our brain's ability to change over our lifetime is called "neuroplasticity." (Use that fancy vocab word to impress people at your next social function!)

## Connection is what brings us calm

When we are young, we are not able to regulate ourselves for two reasons. Our brains are not developed enough, and they are wired to develop optimally through soothing attachment connections.

Human beings crave feeling calm—FROM OTHERS! The body state of equilibrium is where we feel present and open. Safe and free. It is the state where we learn and love best.

---

List three events in your childhood that you remember being emotionally upsetting and whether others were there to help you calm and feel comforted.

1 _____

_____

2 _____

_____

3 _____

_____

What is the moment in your childhood when you felt the most comforted by someone?

_____

_____

_____

_____

_____

_____

_____

_____

_____

_____

_____

_____

If people in your life were only marginally helpful, or no one was there for you at all, write out what you would have wanted someone to do to help you feel safe and calm.

### Allo figures

"Allo" is a Greek word for "other" or nonbiological-family-member relationships. This adaptation where we receive care from people who aren't genetically related to us is a huge part of our human survival.

Were there people in your childhood story who came along and offered you the secure connection that your parents were not able to?

Compare the messages from your family of origin to the messages of these additional caregivers in your life.

Now take a minute and focus on absorbing and believing the more kind and compassionate messages. Just because they didn't come from blood relatives, does not mean they count less. Let them count MORE.

## ATTACHMENT NERD ALERT

Human beings are one of the few species on earth who we can form attachment relationships with people who are not our biological parents. And this is not just the case in foster and adoption settings. We are often given what we need in "chosen" family members in both childhood and adulthood. I have seen many clients with deeply insecure attachment relationships at home, but with a secure internal system because of "allo" caregivers like teachers, community members, grandparents, etc.

### See monkey, do monkey

The human brain is set up to learn from watching others, which means that what you witnessed in your home, even if not directed AT you, impacted your internal world. The way your caregivers interacted with siblings or the other adults in their life had an impact on your understanding of how to relate and connect.

---

What did your caregivers' other relationships—such as with their spouse or siblings—model to you about closeness with others in adulthood?

How did your caregivers talk about themselves and their own needs?

How did your caregivers treat strangers or acquaintances differently than they treated family? How did that affect you?

_____

_____

_____

_____

_____

_____

_____

_____

_____

_____

_____

_____

If you had siblings, in what ways did your caregivers treat you differently than your siblings, including conflict? How did this difference in treatment affect how you felt about yourself?

_____

_____

_____

_____

_____

_____

_____

_____

_____

_____

_____

_____

### Sibling dynamics and security

No two children grow up in the same exact home. Caregivers relate to each child differently, which can affect your emotional security with your caregivers and your siblings. AND sometimes, siblings add to our sense of security through being places where we are seen and cared for.

Put a check mark inside the boxes that ring true for your sibling experience. List out any stories or experiences that were significant to this truth in your story.

☐ My caregiver(s) treated me with more care than one or more of my siblings.

☐ One or more of my siblings was an emotional support for me growing up.

☐ I did not have siblings growing up and this affected me in these positive ways:
_____
_____

☐ My caregiver(s) treated me with less care than one or more of my siblings.

☐ One or more of my siblings was abusive or hurtful with me growing up.

☐ I did not have siblings growing up and it affected me in these negative ways:
_____
_____

### Adolescence and autonomy

When kids enter adolescence, their priority in relationships often shifts from parents to peers. This is called "attachment transfer." While this stage of childhood is exciting in many ways, it is also rife with big feelings and conflicts with parents.

What big feelings do you remember trying to navigate during your teens? How did your parents and/or peers respond?

_____

_____

_____

_____

_____

_____

_____

_____

_____

_____

If you sought out more independence and autonomy, how did your caregivers view that desire? Were you trusted and supported? Or, were your parents suspicious and fearful of your need to venture out?

_____

_____

_____

_____

_____

_____

_____

_____

_____

_____

Who had an influence on you during these years? How did your teenage peer relationships shape your views on your emotions, needs, and ways of connecting?

_____

_____

_____

_____

_____

_____

_____

_____

_____

_____

_____

_____

_____

_____

_____

_____

_____

_____

_____

_____

_____

_____

| SECURE PARENTS | PREOCCUPIED PARENTS | AVOIDANT PARENTS | FEARFUL PARENTS |
|---|---|---|---|
| Tend to trust their teens to make choices and face mistakes. | Tend to enmesh with their teens and try to prevent mistakes. | Tend to address teen behaviors but not feelings. | Tend to take their teens choices as a personal offense and punish harshly. |

## Sexuality and shame

Even more tricky than an adolescent's need for autonomy is what can happen in the dynamic between caregiver and child when the child experiences the emergence of a sexual self.

Many people are taught to fear sexuality or were never given any loving guidance or acceptance at that stage of their own life, so do not know what to say or how to say it.

How did your parents respond to your sexual development? Did they guide you or chide you?

---

---

---

---

---

---

---

---

---

---

---

---

---

---

**SECURE TIP**

Shame about sexuality can be particular potent and hard to share with others, but, shame thrives in secrecy. One incredibly healing thing you can do if you have any trauma around your sexual development is find someone safe and caring to talk to about it. When we are open about the things we feel shame about, we often discover that our story is human and relatable. Which not only reduces our shame feelings but also increases the depth of connection to the people we share with.

What were the messages or lack thereof that your parents sent to you?

_____

_____

_____

_____

_____

_____

_____

_____

_____

_____

_____

_____

_____

_____

_____

How did that affect your attachment to them and reliance on them?

_____

_____

_____

_____

_____

_____

_____

_____

_____

_____

_____

_____

_____

_____

How did your parents respond to these areas of your sexual development?

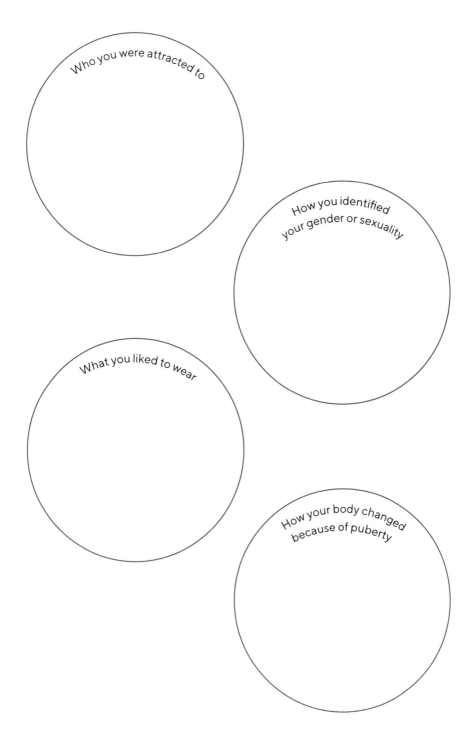

Who you were attracted to

How you identified your gender or sexuality

What you liked to wear

How your body changed because of puberty

### The story of your childhood heart

Take some time and write the story of how your heart felt in relation to your caregivers growing up. Use this space or extra paper to write whatever it is that needs to be acknowledged, and then share this sacred piece of writing with a safe, trustworthy person in your life. And then let yourself receive the care they offer in response.

### Three wishes

One important part of healing our attachment wounds is being able to imagine what it would have looked like if we had gotten our needs met growing up. I want you to take some time to really reflect on what you needed as a child that your caregivers were not able to give you. Make three deeply felt wishes and draw pictures next to your wishes for the younger you that didn't get to have those things in childhood.

**1**

# PART II:
# Where Your Story Ended Up

_____

Here's a theory: Maybe I had
not really been broken this
whole time. Maybe I had
been a human—flawed and
still growing but full of light
nonetheless.

**—STEPHANIE FOO,**
_WHAT MY BONES KNOW:_
_A MEMOIR OF HEALING FROM_
_COMPLEX TRAUMA_

Now that you have done some SERIOUS excavation of your childhood attachment relationships and experiences, it is time to do something similar with your adult attachment experiences.

### Reflect on past and current positive romantic relationships

The security of our attachment strategies can deepen because of being close to people who are securely attached. Think about the ways these types of relationships have contributed to some healing in your journey.

### Reflect on past and current harmful romantic relationships

The security of our attachment strategies can also decrease because of being close to people who use abuse tactics or were extremely dismissive or anxiously intrusive or neglectful in the way they related to us. Think about the ways these types of relationships have added to insecurity in your patterns.

### If you have not had any serious romantic relationships yet

Use this section to reflect on your closest friendships or sibling-type relationships. The ones where you lean on them and they lean on you. I often hear people use the term "she's my person" to describe this type of attachment relationship. Though romance may not be a part here, the bonding is as strong.

# THE CONNECTION BETWEEN EARLY RELATIONSHIPS AND ADULT ATTACHMENTS

Our attachment patterns from childhood become working models in our brains for how we relate to other people. Sometimes our attachment system activates in relationships with very close friends as well, but it activates in the context of the people that we fancy.

Therefore, you can feel such a huge shift in your nervous system when you start seeking (or being sought) out for an intimate romantic relationship. Whatever is stored in your body from your experiences in your growing up years, gets sloshed out onto the people that you are trying to get close to. Your attachment patterns get activated and you utilize whatever strategies you were accustomed to in childhood.

Then, the quality of these romantic relationships adds to the pile of emotional information in your body that adapts your attachment style accordingly. So if you encounter partners who are deeply loving and secure, they can help to heal some of your childhood insecurity. But on the other hand, if you end up with toxic folks who are unkind, abusive, or deeply dismissive of you, it can reinforce and even increase your earlier insecure attachment patterns.

| CHILDHOOD | | | |
|---|---|---|---|
| My caregivers were effective at showing up for my emotional and tender needs. They were consistent and responsive and able to soothe and support me. I learned to trust my body and my needs and to relate to people with authenticity and trust. | My caregivers were hard to predict and would sometimes be there for me, but other times really dropped the ball. I learned to constantly evaluate my attachment figures and to try to adapt my own needs to please them. I learned never to let my guard down. | My caregivers were averse to emotions or incompetent in responding calmly to my needs. I learned not to reach for people in need and instead hide my feelings and distract myself. | My caregivers were scary and posed a threat to my safety emotionally or physically while I was growing up. I learned that close relationships are war zones and that I need to always be survival-focused around people trying to get close to me. |
| ADULTHOOD | | | |
| I feel worthy of love and believe others worthy too. I give freely without questioning myself and I also ask freely when I have a need. I am able to give and receive love without internal complications. | I have been hypervigilant for so long that I do not know how to soothe myself and let love in. Even when things are good in a relationship, I am waiting for the other shoe to drop. This keeps me and my partners on edge and never fully able to melt into security. | I have been ignoring my own feelings for so long that I am not really sure what I feel. When people share their feelings, I move away through humor, dismissal, or avoidance. I struggle to stay connected emotionally with people who want to be close to me. | I have been in survival mode for so long that I see threats in most of my interactions. I have a hard time ever trusting safety and alternate between clinging desperately to people and pushing them away harshly. |

## Grown-up attachments

Make a list of the people with whom you formed attachment relationships in later adolescence and adulthood.

- _____
- _____
- _____

Next to each name, give the person a score for how emotionally caring they were with you.

    5—This person always responded to my needs with loving care.
    4—This person mostly responded to my needs with loving care.
    3—This person sometimes responded to my needs with loving care.
    2—This person rarely responded to my needs with loving care.
    1—This person never responded to my needs with loving care.

Is there a theme of the level of care you were receiving from the people you chose in adulthood?

_____
_____
_____
_____
_____
_____
_____
_____
_____
_____
_____
_____
_____
_____
_____
_____
_____

If you could go back and have a "do-over" with any of these people, what part would you change about how you engaged the other person's needs?

_____

_____

_____

_____

_____

_____

_____

_____

What would you change about how you engaged your own needs in that relationship?

_____

_____

_____

_____

_____

_____

_____

_____

Can you make connections to how you have acted in adult attachment relationships with what you experienced in your relationships in childhood?

_____

_____

_____

_____

_____

_____

_____

_____

## Expectations too high? Or settling for way too little?

We all deserve people capable of meeting our emotional and relational needs and desires. But for those of us who grew up in homes where our needs were not consistently (or ever) met, we often have faulty ideas of what a secure romantic partnership looks like.

Which of these statements do you relate to?

| | |
|---|---|
| **GRANDIOSE EXPECTATIONS (TOO HIGH)** | • If my partner doesn't meet my every single need, I feel betrayed.<br>• I want my partner to know what I need without having to tell them.<br>• I want my partner to heal me.<br>• I want my partner to want the same things as me at the same time.<br>• I think I should always feel happy and connected in my relationship, and I freak out if things aren't going the way I want them to. |
| **SECURE EXPECTATIONS (JUST RIGHT)** | • I do my best to give and receive needs with my partner.<br>• I share my needs openly so my partner can understand them.<br>• I am responsible for healing myself, but I let my partner's love into my heart as a part of that healing.<br>• I accept that there are ups and downs in all relationships and work to repair when things are off course. |
| **INADEQUATE EXPECTATIONS (TOO LOW)** | • I am lucky someone wants to be with me; I don't want to ask for more.<br>• I don't want to burden anyone with what I need, so I stuff them down and pretend I'm fine.<br>• I focus only on what the other person wants and needs and not on myself.<br>• Beggars can't be choosers; I tend to minimize the mistreatment in my relationship. |

Where could you adjust your relationship expectations to be more accepting and compassionate for your romantic partner?

_____

_____

_____

_____

_____

_____

_____

_____

_____

_____

_____

_____

_____

_____

_____

_____

_____

_____

_____

_____

**SECURE TIP**

When you are looking for a relationship or wanting to improve the one you are in, make a list of the relationship qualities that you want, and alongside it, make a list of human imperfections you expect will exist too. When we own our desires at the same time we accept human messiness, we are less likely to settle or get into a relationship that is not a good fit for us.

Where could you adjust your relationship expectations to be more loving and hopeful for yourself and your needs and desires?

Where do you think you got your ideas about what to expect in a romantic relationship?

_____

_____

_____

_____

_____

_____

_____

_____

_____

_____

_____

_____

_____

_____

_____

_____

_____

_____

_____

_____

_____

_____

_____

_____

_____

_____

_____

# ATTACHMENT STRATEGIES AS ANIMAL INSTINCTS

### The Koala Bear

When someone has a Secure attachment strategy, their instinct is to get close to their primary attachment figure and then to feel calm and relaxed through that emotional and physical closeness. Secure adults reach for their partners when they need them, and then feel calmed as a result. For example, koalas feel at home in the arms of their attachment figures.

### The Honey Badger

When someone has an Ambivalent/Preoccupied attachment strategy, their instinct is to constantly scan their primary attachment figure for any possible signs of abandonment and to protest any reassurance. Preoccupied adults constantly reach for their partners but rarely feel soothed by them. Honey badgers are always on the hunt for more honey from their attachment figures.

## The Turtle

When someone has an Avoidant/Dismissive attachment strategy, their instinct is to inhibit awareness of emotions both in themselves and in others. Their brains and nervous systems shut down during distress. Avoidant/Dismissive adults retreat when they are in need and wait out the storm alone. A turtle feels most safe alone in its shell.

## The Teddy/Grizzly Bear

When someone has a Disorganized/Fearful attachment, their instinct is to alternate between clinging desperately, and pushing hard to scare people away. Distress and need trigger intense survival responses that can feel deeply disorienting both to them and to their partners. Disorganized/Unresolved adults often oscillate between "I hate you, go away", and "I will die without you, please don't leave." The teddy bear state makes you appear helpless and small, while the grizzly bear state makes you appear threatening and big.

### Rupture to repair

All relationships have conflict. One major difference between a secure relationship and an insecure relationship is the way that conflict is handled and how quickly and effectively a repair is made. The experiences you had around conflict in your home growing up likely created a template for you that led to your current ways of engaging in conflict in your grown-up attachment relationships.

What was conflict like in your home growing up?

Write about a conflict you had with a caregiver growing up and what you think it taught your body and heart about conflict?

Now write about a conflict with a partner in grown-up life. How was it similar or different?

If you were to handle conflict in a way that made you feel proud in the future, what would you do differently?

_____

_____

_____

_____

_____

_____

_____

_____

_____

_____

_____

_____

_____

_____

_____

_____

_____

_____

## ATTACHMENT NERD ALERT

Receptive versus Defensive Body States: One of the most important skills involved in resolving conflicts is a person's ability to stay calm enough to listen to another person's experience or needs. When our body is in a defensive state, our muscles constrict and our brain shoots out more adrenaline, which makes it physically harder to use our reasoning brain to listen and come back to connection. Signs of a defense/constriction state: Clenched fists, clenched jaw, fast, high heart rate, sweating, not breathing much, feet flat on the ground, pit in stomach. Signs of a receptive/relaxed state: Deep breathing, loose muscles, open hands, steady heart rate, relaxed stomach, relaxed jaw, relaxed shoulders.

## Practicing calmness during conflict

Find a calm, relaxing space to sit in. Spend one to two minutes thinking about an experience where you felt deeply connected to another person. Allow yourself to absorb the calmness and gratitude that came from that experience. Notice what your body feels and the way it responds to that calm, safe memory. Take notes here on what you noticed.

Now I want you to think of a mild conflict you've had in the past (one that was not unsafe or abusive). When you notice your body starting to constrict or tighten, remember the calm state you conjured up from before . . . focus on creating those same calm body sensations while deep breathing and saying kind things to yourself to change yourself from a defensive place to a receptive place.

_____

_____

_____

_____

_____

_____

_____

_____

Write down what changed in your perspective on that fight as you calmed your body while thinking about it. Does the fight feel like less of a big deal? Do you feel more empowered to speak your perspective? Do you feel like you will be able to react more effectively?

_____

_____

_____

_____

_____

_____

_____

**SECURE TIP**

When having a conflict, focus on calming your body BEFORE trying to get your point across or trying to receive the other person's message. This practice of calming your body during conflict will be a major game changer in your ability to reconnect with loved ones during tricky moments. Like anything you learn though, you will have to practice it.

## Separation space station

Attachment is about closeness, right? Well yes and no. It is about a quality of closeness that allows us to venture freely into the world because we know we have a safe, secure, base to return to. But if you didn't have loving, stable caregivers as a base growing up, you might react to space travel (separation from our partners) in the extreme.

Perhaps you find it anxiety-provoking, even for short periods of time. Maybe you find being close to people overwhelming and often want to float out into the universe solo.

| SECURE | PREOCCUPIED | AVOIDANT | DISORGANIZED |
|---|---|---|---|
| Tend to miss their partners but feel secure even in separation | Tend to find space and separation threatening and deeply distressing | Tend to find space and separation calming and are most at ease there | Tend to project abandonment or malintent onto partners in absence |

Draw a picture or write a poem about what separation and physical space from your people feel like in your body and brain:

### Protest protest protest

There is a time and a place for protest. But a secure loving relationship isn't one of them. To "protest" is a coping skill many people develop in which they refuse to be soothed. It "works" because if you are always making a stink, someone has to stay close to you to fix it. Which makes you feel safe(ish). But it also makes you feel like you are stressing people out. Because you are.

The key antidote to protest is learning how to receive comfort and reassurance.

---

### Let's Practice

I want you to write down two to four fearful thoughts that have taken up space in your romantic relationships in the past or present, despite never actually coming to fruition.

1 _____

2 _____

3 _____

4 _____

Now I want you to make a list of all the things that your partner or ex-partner(s) or friends said and did to reassure you.

_____

_____

_____

_____

_____

_____

_____

_____

_____

_____

_____

_____

Next, rewrite the fears in teeny tiny letters below. THEN over the fears, I want you to rewrite all the reassuring pieces of data in big letters to symbolize their importance and truth in your heart over the fears you carried from the past.

**SECURE TIP**

Start a Honey Journal. Every time a partner does something that makes you feel loved, nurtured, or respected, take note of it in your Honey Journal. Let that journal fill up and take up space in your mind and your story about yourself and the love you deserve.

# ATTACHMENT NERD ALERT

Did you know that the WAY we narrate our past attachment relationships can indicate what current attachment category we fall into? Mary Main and Eric Hesse at the University of California, Berkeley, created a tool called the Adult Attachment Interview (AAI).

This is what the research found:

If you have an AMBIVALENT/PREOCCUPIED attachment pattern:
You tend to alternate between speaking in present and past tense when talking about past attachment experiences. You tend to use aggrandizing descriptions of your pain and distress.

If you have an AVOIDANT/DISMISSIVE attachment pattern:
You tend to lack details when you talk about the past and instead use vague language when talking about past attachment experience. You tend to use euphemisms for your pain and distress to downplay it.

If you have a DISORGANIZED/UNRESOLVED attachment pattern:
You are unable to tell a coherent narrative about your past attachment experiences without shutting down or getting heightened and hyper-aroused and upset. Your story is too triggering to tell.

If you have a SECURE/AUTONOMOUS attachment pattern:
You are able to talk about both the good things and the bad things from your past attachment experiences in depth of detail and coherence without becoming overly triggered.

# BREAKING UP IS HARD TO DO . . .

Breakups are awful. But they are part of MOST people's attachment journey. Sigh. We have to address them, even though it can be painful to bring them up.

Here are some definitions to help you think about this part of your story.

### Ghosting
When someone you are sharing a special connection with chooses to stop contacting you or responding to you without any explanation or closure.

### The walking dead
The people you have lost a close relationship with but who are technically still alive and out in the world.

### Over it
When you feel deep resolved peace about the ending of a relationship.

### Not over it
When you continue to feel big, icky, overwhelming feelings when you think about an ex-partner or friend. The disturbance in your body has not yet subsided.

### Ghosting and the walking dead

I have personally never seen a ghost, but I have absolutely seen how bad relationships and breakups haunt the daylights out of people. I can also tell you that you don't ghost-bust your past relationships by trying to forget them. They will just keep coming up through the cracks in your heart.

If you are feeling haunted by a past traumatic breakup or past relationship, these questions will explore the unfinished business you feel.

---

Make a list of all your breakups. (I counted my own breakups while writing this so that you would not feel alone. Twelve breakups between high school and meeting my husband . . . My husband only had one.)

| | |
|---|---|
| _____ | _____ |
| _____ | _____ |
| _____ | _____ |
| _____ | _____ |
| _____ | _____ |
| _____ | _____ |

Now cross off the ones that feel resolved. They are the ones that you can think about without your insides going topsy turvy. Those ones aren't haunting you.

Go through the list and ask yourself whether the relationship itself was traumatic or the way it ended was traumatic. Was it both? Write about the breakups here.

If it was the relationship, call a friend who knew you when you were still in the relationship. Ask them to give you some time to talk through that relationship and help you identify why you are still struggling with the ghost of it. What do you wish could have been different about how the relationship played out and ultimately ended?

Then, on a separate piece of paper, write an encouraging and caring letter to your broken heart. What do you need to hear about these past relationships and their endings so that your heart can feel healed and hopeful to move forward? Be as kind and generous as you would to a dear friend.

**SECURE TIP**

When we lose people, we often feel ashamed. The key to resolving that loss is by recognizing that we did not deserve the loss and that we are deserving of love.

# PEOPLE-PLEASING AS A SURVIVAL SKILL

If you grew up in a family where a parent or a sibling was highly reactive, or if you fell into a brutally abusive relationship later in adulthood, you may have developed one or both of these codependent coping skills to survive.

Fawning is when you are overly positive, generous, and kind to other people in hopes that it will keep the target off your head. You learned that if you constantly pleased this toxic person(s) from your past that they would aim their rage at you less (not never, just less).

Responsibility dysmorphia is what happens as a result. After fawning as a survival instinct, you became adept at taking on other people's responsibilities and believing that it was YOUR actions that controlled THEIR behaviors and emotional responses. Your idea of your responsibility is out of whack.

## How did you people-please?

People-pleasing is a barrier to a secure attachment because it is riddled with fear and it blocks the opportunity for honesty and equity in a relationship. Only people with deep narcissistic patterns want you to serve and please them, which means they are not yet capable of a secure attachment.

Make a list of people whose anger and rage necessitated your fawning or taking responsibility for other people's feelings and actions.

_____

_____

_____

_____

_____

_____

_____

_____

_____

_____

Make a list of past experiences you took responsibility for that you had no power to change. For example, believing that it was your fault when a parent erupted at you. Or feeling like avoiding your partner's accusations was your job. Or believing you needed to be a perfect partner so a sweetheart wouldn't cheat on you.

_____

_____

_____

_____

_____

_____

_____

_____

SECURELY ATTACHED

Imagine that you are putting other people's responsibility back on them. Blow those responsibilities into an imaginary balloon and let them float out into space and away from you. If it was not something you could control, you do not need to keep holding on to it.

SECURE
TIP

If you cannot read someone's face to tell if they are receiving what you feel, they may have an Avoidant attachment strategy. Ask what they are feeling, because it may be that they are receiving your emotions but just don't know how to show it.

### Hope is a real booger

I know we tend to think of hope as all unicorns and rainbows, but actually it is some seriously heavy stuff. When we hope, we are taking a risk. This is why so many of us are tempted to forgo hope and succumb to our armchairs, Instagrams, and TikTok accounts rather than reach for the people we are wanting more closeness with. But the thing is . . . hope is a heaviness worth holding. It is necessary for taking steps forward.

What would it look like to hope for more in your close relationships?

What are you afraid might happen if you do hope?

What do you think will happen if you do not?

_____

_____

_____

_____

_____

_____

What are messages of hope that friends and loved ones have made on your behalf?

_____

_____

_____

_____

_____

_____

_____

_____

_____

_____

_____

_____

_____

_____

_____

_____

_____

Did you know that the way the people in your life "mirror" your emotional states affects whether you feel secure with them? If you are sad and someone smiles at you, it IS NOT comforting, it is mis-attuned. Just like if you are full of joy and someone makes a frowny face in your direction.

We long to see our emotional states reflected on the faces of people we are close to. Other people's mirror of our emotional state signals to our nervous system that they are receiving what we feel, which makes us feel less alone, which then helps our system to calm. (There is a whole theory called Polyvagal Theory, which posits that we have an entire nerve dedicated to this signaling between faces.)

Dr. Ed Tronick, in his work through the Still Face Experiment, identified how mirroring affects infants and how a blank face is actually deeply distressing to our nervous systems. If you google the Still Face research, grab a tissue, because it is surprising how heartbreaking it is to watch a child deal with a blank face from a caregiver for only one minute.

### What's your worthiness level?

Trick question! There is no system of evaluating worth! Did you know that? You're human, so you're worthy of secure love and affection! PERIOD. But that doesn't mean that you FEEL worthy. And how we feel about our worth has a huge impact on who we choose, what we settle for, and whether we advocate for what we want and need in relationships.

What messages have you gotten so far in your relationships about your worth and what you deserve?

If you were to fully embrace the idea that you are worthy and deserving of love, what would you do differently in your past, present, and future relationships?

_____

_____

_____

_____

_____

_____

_____

_____

_____

_____

_____

_____

_____

_____

_____

_____

_____

_____

_____

_____

_____

_____

Reflect on all the good traits you have that you bring into a relationship. Are you generous? Do you say sorry easily? Are you playful? Or thoughtful? Or do you make a superb lasagna? Reflect on how your presence is a gift to others. If you struggle to find kind things to say about your value in relationships, ask a friend or two and see what they have to say.

### Marie Kondo your past relationship stuff

Do you know Marie, the home-organization mastermind? She has a person pick up every single item in their home and ask, "Do I need this? Does this bring me joy?" If not, to the thrift store it goes.

In a similar vein, when it comes to the things that we experienced in our romantic relationships that we keep inside our minds and bodies, it helps to notice what remains after a relationship fails (or never comes to be) and sort through whether there is anything worthy of keeping for the journey forward. Do we need it? Does it bring us joy?

What are some memories you want to keep from past relationships that make you feel good about yourself and the way you loved or were loved?

What are some hurtful things past partners did or said that you want to leave behind?

Are there things that you did or said that no longer represent the way you want to identify as a partner and a person?

_____

_____

_____

_____

_____

_____

_____

_____

_____

_____

_____

When you think about your past relationships, what do you learn that you want to keep as a lesson moving forward?

_____

_____

_____

_____

_____

_____

_____

_____

_____

_____

_____

_____

### Self-lovin' in the oven

Do you know who the person is that you spend the most time with? It's YOU, silly goose! And if you are the person that you spend the most time with, then your relationship with yourself is going to have a big impact on how you feel about yourself and therefore how secure you can be in your other relationships.

If you treated yourself as if you were your own TRUE LOVE ...

How would you talk to yourself differently?

_____
_____
_____
_____
_____
_____
_____
_____
_____
_____

How would you treat your body differently?

_____
_____
_____
_____
_____
_____
_____
_____
_____
_____
_____
_____
_____

Who would you spend less time around? More?

What habits would you start? Quit?

What dreams would you work to fulfill?

_____

_____

_____

_____

_____

_____

_____

What daily acts of kindness would you do?

_____

_____

_____

_____

_____

_____

_____

_____

_____

_____

_____

**SECURE TIP**

Do those things you brainstormed above for yourself! The more love you feel from you, the more securely you will believe yourself worthy of love from others.

## To the land of what if . . .

You have done some serious work reflecting on your relational journey and what attachment relationships have been like for you. Now it is time to imagine what it is that you want in your future.

What if you could share your needs without fear? What would you share with a sweetheart?

_____

_____

_____

_____

_____

_____

_____

_____

_____

_____

What if you could experience full affection and care from another person? How would you want them to express their love to you?

_____

_____

_____

_____

_____

_____

_____

_____

_____

_____

_____

_____

What if you could honor the standards you hold for how you want to be treated? What things would be on that list?

_____

_____

_____

_____

_____

_____

_____

_____

_____

_____

What values would you want to share with your partner or have your partner deeply respect in you?

_____

_____

_____

_____

_____

_____

_____

_____

_____

**SECURE TIP**

When you resolve your early insecurity, you are no longer seeking love to be worthy, but instead looking for relationships that are worthy of what you want.

## PART III:
# Where Your Story Is Heading

_____

Love is not just a passion spark between two people; there is infinite difference between falling in love and standing in love.

**—IRVIN YALOM,**
_LOVE'S EXECUTIONER AND OTHER TALES OF PSYCHOTHERAPY_

This section is designed to get you practicing secure ways of loving. This is complex because everyone is in a unique life circumstance. You will use this section differently depending on your current relationship status.

### If You Are in Attachment Heaven

For those of you who are in relationships that feel secure already (romantic or close friendships) or are at the beginning of a brand-new relationship that doesn't feel tarnished or complex yet, use Where Your Story Is Heading as a bolster to that security. Take the things that are going well and grow them. Look for the things that could still be improved and work on them!

### If You Are in Attachment Purgatory

For those of you who are currently not in a romantic relationship (but wanting one), you will want to practice these things with the people who currently are your closest connections. That could be friends or family members. Anytime the word "partner" gets used in the text, substitute it for "my people," and work on loving them as securely as you can.

### If You Are in Attachment Hell

For those of you that are in painful relationship dynamics at this time in your journey, I want you to do your best to be loving and kind, but not pour out all this loving goodness toward people who are harmful to you. Instead, focus on giving this love to safe connections and people who are mutually invested in your well-being, even if that isn't the person you are partnered with. (It's probably a good idea to get a therapist on board too.)

# THE PRACTICE OF SECURE LOVE

The attachment research is clear that when people reflect on their childhoods and past relationships, they are one huge step closer to earning a secure pattern of relating. (You did this in Part I and II! Hooray!)

Next step: Learn and apply secure ways of relating to others!

I like to think of these two different steps of learning a secure attachment as the demolition and rebuild. The demolition is messier and often reveals rotted walls or asbestos ceilings that we didn't anticipate. The rebuild is both fun and hard. It is fun because you are picking out the furnishings and tiles and designs that you want in your remodel, but hard because sometimes things take longer than expected, or parts are back ordered, or you're just so used to the old stuff that it takes a hot minute to put up the new drywall.

I promise, though, at the end of your attachment remodel, it will be worth it. It is hard while you are doing it, but in the end, you will be free to love in a way you have likely never felt before.

# EIGHT TRAITS OF A SECURE ATTACHMENT PATTERN

When we look at the qualities that we want to develop in ourselves to create secure relationships, it is likely that there are areas where we excel and areas where we need to grow.

---

Fill in the star for every trait below that you feel confident is well developed in yourself; fill in the triangle next to the ones that need improvement; and fill in a square next to the ones that REALLY need work. (We all have stars, triangles, and squares on our lists!)

**Caring** ☆△□
A person with a secure attachment pattern offers emotional and practical care to the people they are close to, without condition or expectation.

**Receptive** ☆△□
A person with a secure attachment pattern is open to the emotional needs and states of the people they are close to, even in hard times.

**Curious** ☆△□
A person with a secure attachment pattern wants to know and learn more about the people they are close to, no matter how long they have known them.

**Accountable** ☆△□
A person with a secure attachment pattern is capable of owning their mistakes and making repairs with the people they are close to.

**Responsive** ☆△□
A person with a secure attachment pattern is available and quickly responsive to the tender and emotional needs of their people.

**Equitable** ☆△□
A person with a secure attachment pattern is concerned with everyone getting what they need (including themselves) and no one being left with a disproportionate amount of labor in the relationship tasks.

**Honest** ☆△□
A person with a secure attachment pattern is authentic and shares their true thoughts and needs with their partners.

**Compassionate** ☆△□
A person with a secure attachment pattern has a tender heart toward themselves and others.

# THERE IS NO SCOREBOARD IN SECURE ATTACHMENT

So many people are stuck in an insecure scarcity mindset. This mindset leads to constantly keeping score in your relationship. Who did the dishes last? Who says I love you first? Who spends the most on groceries? Who initiates sex more? This mindset feels like protection, but it is damaging to the relationship.

The goal isn't to have a partner who does everything the exact same way and amount as you. The goal is to find someone who shows how they are as devoted and committed to the relationship as you are.

Write about the ways in which you can focus less on what each person is doing on the scoreboard. How does your partner complement your strengths and weaknesses?

_____

_____

_____

_____

_____

_____

_____

_____

_____

_____

_____

_____

_____

_____

_____

_____

_____

**SECURE TIP**

A secure mindset says, "I want to give and receive care from my partner and will trust that we are both doing the best we can and that it will all come out in the laundry (pun intended), even in the end."

Instead of a scoreboard, think of every act of love you give and every act of love you receive as adding to a beautiful, quilted tapestry. The more you put on, the more beautiful it becomes. Sometimes you will put on more patches, sometimes your partner will be the one adding more to the quilt, but it will still be the same quilt. Fill in the boxes below for some of the patches you or a partner have added to the beauty of a relationship quilt.

## 5:1

According to the Gottman Institute, one of the most world-renowned relationship research organizations, this ratio is a very important one to remember: 5:1. According to their scientific findings, stable and secure relationships have five positive interactions for every one negative interaction DURING conflict. This is established through a culture of expressing kindness and love to one another.

So, moving forward into a secure style of relating, you want to work on creating a pattern of generosity and connection that will help you keep your gloves on when the inevitable conflicts arise.

---

Here is a list of positive interaction ideas to reflect on and use as you work to deepen the security in your relationships. If you have a partner, which ones do you think your partner would like? Which ones might need a little practice from you?

- Give a compliment

- Blow an air kiss

- Celebrate an accomplishment together

- Do a favor

- Be on time for each other

- Laugh at a joke

- Make them some coffee

- Be goofy

- Hold hands

- Fall asleep saying I love you

- Give a hug or a kiss

- Wear a scent they like

- Let them comfort you in hard moments

- Do a chore that isn't yours

- Read an article they asked you to

- Buy a fav candy

- Tell them an important story from your day

- Write a love note

- Offer physical affection or intimacy

- Say I like you

- REALLY listen

- Flirt with them

- Say thank you

- Be empathetic to their feelings

- Acknowledge their work

- Offer a back rub

- Brag about them in front of others

- Snuggle on the couch

- Make them breakfast in bed

- Watch their show with them

**SECURE TIP**

Instead of focusing on how many positive things your partner is doing for you, focus on your efforts and what you are doing to create connection in your relationship. When we focus on our part, it gives us serenity instead of fixating on what we cannot change.

## When you feel disconnected, reach for your person

Disconnection is a normal part of even the healthiest relationships. It will happen even if you've juiced up your connection with lots of positive interactions. We get out of sync with our sweethearts, and they get out of sync with us. The key is how we handle those moments.

When you feel disconnected from your important people do you tend to:
- Hunker down and isolate?
- Get angry and agitate?
- Freak out and perseverate?

These old habits are insecure and will only prolong your disconnection . . .

Instead, remember this:
- Calmly reach and reconnect

Write out two to three sentences you can use to reach for your partner the next time you are trying to reconnect:

_____

_____

_____

_____

_____

_____

_____

What are ways that your partner can effectively reach for you? A gentle touch? A kind word? Is there a certain phrase or action that helps you know they need you?

_____

_____

_____

_____

_____

_____

_____

## Respond, don't take it on

One of the most important roles that our attachment relationships hold is the role of soothing and support. The strongest and most secure romantic attachment relationships are built on a foundation of care.

A securely attached person shows up in the hard moments and shows care but does not try to fix anything or take anything on. Their own stability is separate from the other person's emotional state.

Think of the spectrum like this:

| NON-RESPONSIVE | EMPATHETIC AND GROUNDED | HYPER-RESPONSIVE |
|---|---|---|
| *Too separate/ feels non-caring* | *Just right* | *Too enmeshed/ feels intrusive* |

Do you have relationships where you tend toward the nonresponsive end of the spectrum? Do you flee or shut down? How do you think that impacts those relationships?

_____

_____

_____

_____

_____

_____

_____

_____

_____

_____

_____

_____

_____

_____

_____

_____

_____

_____

Do you have relationships where you tend toward the hyper-responsive end of the spectrum? How do you think that impacts those relationships?

_____

_____

_____

_____

_____

_____

_____

_____

_____

_____

_____

_____

_____

_____

_____

_____

_____

_____

_____

_____

_____

_____

 **ATTACHMENT NERD ALERT**

In the Strange Situation research, there is a score that babies get for proximity seeking. The babies that run at a full sprint and climb up their caregiver's bodies independently get the highest score in that category. Reaching for your people in distress does not make you needy, it makes you attachment-savvy!

When have people responded too far on either end of the spectrum to your needs? How did that impact you?

What do you think you could do to move closer to the sweet spot of grounded empathy?

# IS THIS CONFLICT?
# OR ABUSE?

This is a VERY important question to ask yourself in any relationship you are in. We can get caught in abusive cycles with bosses, friends, family, and even coworkers. But no abusive relationship is as potentially dangerous as one between romantic partners.

If you find yourself in frequent discord and stress because of your relationship, you want to evaluate whether you are working through things (because all relationships have hard seasons that take effort and feel painful), or STUCK in a cycle that does not improve, and, likely, gets worse over time.

Abuse starts and ends in our mentality. It is driven by a belief system that goes like this:

"I should get what I want, when I want it, without any pushback from anyone. If I do not get it, then I feel justified to intentionally create pain in another person to punish them and regain my sense of control."

If you or your partner has this mentality, then the cycle will only end when the person with the mentality sees their mindset and history of abusive actions as a problem they want to solve.

Unfortunately, folks with this mindset have a very low recovery rate. If you do identify this pattern in yourself or your partner, the next step is individual counseling with someone who specializes in abuse.

# UNSAFE PATTERNS

Here is a list of abusive behaviors and mindsets to be wary of in yourself and your partners (especially if patterns get worse over time).

| | |
|---|---|
| **EMOTIONAL ABUSE** | • Name calling<br>• Telling demeaning jokes<br>• Making frequent accusations<br>• Gaslighting<br>• Isolating you from friends<br>• Controlling your choices<br>• Treating you like a child<br>• Posturing to be bigger than you<br>• Controlling your finances |
| **PHYSICAL ABUSE** | • Hitting<br>• Slapping<br>• Punching<br>• Kicking<br>• Damaging property<br>• Strangulation<br>• Wielding weapons<br>• Blocking an exit<br>• Forcing drugs or restricting medications |
| **SEXUAL ABUSE** | • Forcing sexual acts<br>• Coercion<br>• Touching you when you don't want it<br>• Pressuring acts you aren't comfortable with<br>• Guilting you for saying no<br>• Cheating<br>• Being rough without explicit enthusiastic consent<br>• Insulting your body during sex<br>• Sexually harassing you around other people or alone |

### Ahoy! Conflict discovery ahead!

In contrast to the previous section, within safe dynamics conflict is an opportunity to discover your matey! (See what I did there? Arrrrrrr.) Truly, your partner is an incredibly complex being who has miles and miles of undiscovered land. When you enter into a conflict, it is an opportunity to learn something new about them. And a chance for them to learn about you too.

Think of a recent conflict you have had with your partner or someone close to you. What did this conflict reveal to you about the person you were in conflict with? It could be about their needs, their life story, or the way their brain is wired.

_____

_____

_____

_____

_____

_____

_____

_____

_____

_____

_____

_____

_____

_____

_____

_____

_____

_____

_____

_____

_____

_____

_____

_____

_____

_____

_____

_____

_____

_____

_____

_____

_____

_____

_____

_____

_____

_____

_____

_____

_____

_____

_____

_____

**SECURE TIP**

When you are in a conflict, ask yourself the question: what is the conflict asking me/us to discover? THEN when the conflict is over, come up with a name for the fight. You can make it funny or relate the name to the theme you were learning. It makes it seem less scary and solidifies something you did and learned together.

## The boundary lands

All healthy relationships have boundaries.

ALL. OF. THEM. I promise you are not being mean to your partner or friends by having limits and a need for specific boundaries. What boundaries you need to have are based on your needs and your partner's needs.

Reflect on what boundaries you need to establish in the following categories:

**Financial**

_____
_____
_____
_____
_____

**Use of your things**

_____
_____
_____
_____
_____

**Discussion of certain subjects**

_____
_____
_____
_____
_____

Family dynamics

_____

_____

_____

_____

_____

Your shared sexual intimacy

_____

_____

_____

_____

Connections with other people outside the relationship

_____

_____

_____

_____

Privacy and what can be shared with others in your lives

_____

_____

_____

_____

Anything else?

_____

_____

_____

_____

_____

## ◯◯ ATTACHMENT
## ❤ NERD ALERT

Did you know that when you are emotionally attuned or connected to another person, you both experience in your brains what is called limbic resonance?

When you receive another person's feeling state, and allow it in, your brain lights up in a similar region, creating the effect of "feeling felt." Or "empathy," as we more commonly call it.

This science of empathy is still being studied through neuroimaging and we still have so much to learn, but this image of letting your brain light up in a particular synchronicity to someone else's brain state makes this attachment nerd very warm and fuzzy.

# RISKY BUSINESS

I don't have to tell you what you already know. It is risky to love. There is no way around that. When we let ourselves bond to someone, we are put in a precarious position to lose.

We all must reckon with this fear and live with it. The key is understanding that it is normal to feel the risk and fear, and to not try to obliterate it through a false sense of control. (No, tracking your partner's GPS location does not make your relationship safer.)

You likely already know how to do this. Let me explain.

When you get into a car, you know that you could end up in an accident. But you have to get into a car to function in modern life (or a train or a bus). So you see the risk, and say to yourself, "Well, I sure as heck hope that doesn't happen, because I have to get to work."

You buckle your seat belt. You put your phone down (please!), and you mitigate the risk by keeping your eyes on the road. But you get in that vehicle, and you go.

Same with love. Yes, you could get into a love accident, but you may not. And in the meantime, it would stall your life to stay where you are and not get moving on love. Obsessing about how you might get hurt will not protect you, it will just get in your way.

### Risk reflections

And while I 100 percent agree with the notion that "it is better to have loved and lost than never to have loved at all," I also understand that it can still feel scary scary scary. Reflect on ways you might be getting in your own way.

What are you scared will happen if you let your guard down and trust someone fully?

Do you hold back on the love you give to people to protect yourself?

_____

_____

_____

_____

_____

_____

_____

_____

_____

Do you put up walls to prevent the love that others give from fully getting in?

_____

_____

_____

_____

_____

_____

_____

_____

_____

**SECURE TIP**

Nothing can prepare you for loss. It is awful. But if you have done all you can to live fully in the moment, you at least know you gave it your all and there was nothing more for you to do. So loving radically, fully, and without guardedness will protect you from having to navigate loss and regret simultaneously.

## Being an emotionally TRUSTWORTHY partner

When we think of trust, we often think of how someone might nefariously trick or harm us (which I would consider abuse), but trust has deeper roots than just being safe.

Someone can be safe (not going to actively harm you) but not be trustworthy (not going to actively catch you or hold you) in how they respond to your tender emotional needs.

---

Use this rating scale to reflect on the following three domains of being emotionally trustworthy. If you are currently unpartnered, think of situations with close friends.

1 — Oh, crap, calling my therapist now
2 — Making myself an improvement plan
3 — Middle of the road: a bit longer to go
4 — Pretty darn good, but fine-tuning to do
5 — Enthusiastic pat on my back

- **PRESENCE:** Do you show up with your whole self and presence with your partner, both in their pains and joys?

  _____

  _____

- **RELIABILITY:** Do you follow through on your word and show up consistently in both big and small ways?

  _____

  _____

- **CONSIDERATION:** Do you spend time and energy reflecting on your person, what they feel and need, and how you can offer them love in ways that are specific to their preferences?

  _____

  _____

### Being an emotionally TRUSTING partner

If you grew up with a secure attachment, you likely assume the best of intentions in others, unless someone is overtly acting shady.

But if you grew up with any of the insecure attachment mentalities, you likely conflate intention and impact. So if someone hurts you in some way, you look for some clue that they did it on purpose (the only way you feel valid in feeling pain), or that they don't care about you (a message you may have internalized earlier), instead of being curious about what was going on for them.

---

Reflect on a time you may have conflated intention and impact.

Trust is a feeling that develops over time and through repeated patterns. If you want to be trustworthy with a partner, make efforts and sustain them over time.

# THEORY OF MIND

Did you know that your typical assumptions of why people do and feel the way they do is sculpted by your early attachment experiences? It is called your "theory of mind," and it is largely about how you view the intentions of others.

Part of being a secure partner now is putting trust in the people you choose to keep close to you, and letting them be the authority on their intentions, even in painful moments. To do this, you need two very important emotional boundaries:

1   Intention can only be named or validated by each individual person. No one can tell you what you intend, and you can't tell anyone else what they intend.

2   Pain is valid whether pain was intended. (So something IMPACTS even if it was an accident).

Think of a conflict you've had as an adult.
*   Have you ever ascribed ill intent to someone amid a fight?
*   Have you struggled to believe your pain was legitimate in a situation where you knew the other person meant no harm?
*   Do you take accountability for the impact of your actions even when you did not mean to hurt?
*   If you have struggled to take accountability in the past, what are some ways you could take accountability in the future?

**SECURE TIP**

All pain is valid regardless of its source. When we acknowledge our own pain and the pain of others, we become more deeply connected to each other.

## Being an emotionally grounded partner

Our attachment relationships can be incredibly healing spaces. They can help mend old wounds and alter our beliefs about ourselves and our futures. BUT, they do not absolve us in our ultimate responsibility to ensure that we are taking care of ourselves.

When we do not take care of ourselves, we put our partners in a precarious position. Either they have to watch us suffer and feel powerless, or they can get enmeshed in our problematic patterns and feel responsible to save or rescue us, which will ultimately end in resentment and disconnection.

What active steps can you take in the domains below to ensure that you are as grounded as you can be in yourself? Write examples for each.

• Feeding your heart with other relationships and connections

_____

_____

• Taking time to do things that make you feel alive and hopeful

_____

_____

• Moving your body to keep your physical heart strong

_____

_____

• Participating in things to make the world a better place

_____

_____

**SECURE TIP**

We all long for secure places where we can express our most tender emotions and be met with empathy. The most effective partners are 1) highly responsive and 2) highly differentiated (a big word that just means grounded and calm).

• Taking care of spiritual and intellectual needs and creating rhythms around those

_____

_____

• Drinking water and giving your body nourishment from food

_____

_____

• Resting

_____

_____

• Taking care of your financial well-being

_____

_____

• Surrounding yourself with people who are kind

_____

_____

**SECURE TIP**

The more efforts you make to take care of and nurture yourself, the more worthy you will feel of receiving love from your partner.

### Being generous

Our sweethearts and closest friends are the people who see us at our best and our worst. They see us in our most put-together outfit days, and our least laundered sweatpants days. Because we are at our most comfortable within our intimate attachment relationships, it can be easy to slip into a critical space focusing on the things that annoy us.

While annoyance and critique are definitely part of a normal secure partnership, chronic annoyance and critique are not. Generosity is a mental choice, a commitment to making room for our partners to be real people with flaws, and to respond to those flaws with gentleness and love.

---

Who do you know that is generous with their sweetheart? What do you see them do that you want to learn to emulate?

What do you give easily in terms of a relationship? (money, affection, apologies, time, gifts, acts of service, kind words, etc.?)

_____

_____

_____

_____

_____

_____

_____

_____

_____

_____

What do you struggle to be generous with? Why do you think that is?

_____

_____

_____

_____

_____

_____

_____

Make a plan for one area of generosity you want to be known for and practice well.

**SECURE TIP**

The stingier you are with your love, resources, and compassion, the more likely it is that you have a "scarcity mindset," which means that you fear if you give away your resources, you will have less. But in a secure relationship, the more you give, the more you get. The generous spirit multiplies and creates a dynamic of giving. There will be enough to go around and you will not have to hoard anything to survive.

## Being a nurturing partner

Nurture is one of the most important pieces of a secure partnership. Nurture is a gentle, present, loving response to another person's pain, stress, fear, or insecurity. Drawing upon Gary Chapman's idea of the five love languages, reflect on these categories using these guiding questions:

Do I give this type of nurture? Have my past or present partners wanted more of it from me? What goal can I make in this area to help me give it more often? What past trauma or pain or inexperience might be in my way?

**Nurturing touch**

**Nurturing words**

## Nurturing acts of service

_____

_____

_____

_____

_____

_____

_____

_____

_____

## Nurturing gifts

_____

_____

_____

_____

_____

_____

_____

_____

_____

## Nurturing quality time

_____

_____

_____

_____

_____

_____

_____

_____

_____

### Being an open partner

Everyone has needs. Asking for what we need feels vulnerable, but it is a part of being open.

Make a list of needs you have not verbalized in your past or present relationship that you would like to be heard and met.

**1**

**2**

**3**

**4**

**5**

# MIND READING IS OVERRATED

If you had parents who ignored your nonverbal cues or misread them (a.k.a. could not accurately read your mind) when you were little, then you are likely to believe that your needs ONLY matter if someone notices them without you asking. So you feel dependent on others naming your need for you, often growing crusty and bitter when they don't.

If you had parents who read your nonverbal cues (a.k.a. could read your mind when you were little at the appropriate stage of life to do so), you are likely to believe your needs matter and share them as soon as you have them, instead of waiting for someone to notice them.

The secure action is always to SAY WHAT YOU NEED and not to wait for someone to figure it out. And a secure partner . . . will try to meet your need, not try to figure it out before you ask.

**SECURE TIP**

If you are struggling to believe that what you need matters, write it down on a piece of paper and imagine that a friend passed it to you as a need. What would you feel about them bringing that same thing to you? Probably valid right? It's valid for you too then!

### Leaning on your village

If we have learned anything from the attachment research, it is this: Secure human beings rely on other people to help them regulate and thrive throughout life. And that security goes beyond our primary attachment figure and into a mindset of connection with others.

Who are the people in your life you can lean on when tough times come for you and your partner?

_____

_____

_____

_____

_____

_____

_____

_____

_____

_____

Who are the people in your life you can learn from to continue in your quest to give and receive a secure loving attachment experience?

_____

_____

_____

_____

_____

_____

_____

_____

_____

_____

What authors/speakers/resources can you draw upon as well?

_____

_____

_____

_____

_____

_____

_____

_____

_____

_____

_____

_____

_____

_____

_____

_____

_____

# GROWTH MINDSET

You did it!!!! (I am showering down trillions of imaginary balloons and confetti all over you without creating any more micro-plastic waste!)

You made it through this entire process and have moved mountains in your attachment journey to be at the end of this workbook. So good.

So what now?

Outside of these pages, you will continue to be faced with the dance of your past, present, and future. You will continue to learn new things about yourself, and new things about love itself and the people you are giving love to and receiving love from. You will have moments of feeling FAR more secure than you did previously, and you will have moments when you slip back into your old neural networks and start acting in ways that you thought you had let go. That's normal. Don't beat yourself up; just recognize it as a chance to deepen your growth. Be curious. Why is this coming up? How can I care for myself and move into a secure strategy?

Here are some last tips for how to use this book as you continue onwards in your attachment story:

1   This book is now an emotional memory album you can share with close people.

2   I hope you will share the stories and insights you labored to put into this book with the trusted people who are lucky enough to be close and intimate with you. Your story, even in its painful parts, is what makes you YOU. And your resilience in your story is truly remarkable and worth sharing.

3   Part III can be used as an instruction manual when you feel lost in a relationship.

4   When new relationships arise, you can use Part III to reference how you are doing and what you are improving and working to do better! We all need reminders from time to time.

5   You can use the work you've done as an accountability resource to check in on your progress and stay with this work.

Once a year, whip this bad girl out and review it. Highlight the things that you successfully improved over the year and add notes for review the next year.

# My Closing Love Letter to You ...

It is sort of on the hokey side to say "I am proud of you" to someone that I may not have ever had the honor of meeting. But I have been doing this work long enough to know that what you just accomplished took courage, energy, time, pain, and dedication. Healing your attachment wounds and learning secure ways of connecting is WORK.

So I am proud of you.

And I am honored that you trusted me with your heart to guide you through some tricky stuff.

I hope more than anything it has helped you understand more about yourself and why you have functioned the way you have in relationships. And in turn, that understanding can act as a bridge to freedom from the pain of the past, into hope for good things in your present and future relationships.

Your attachment journey is a lifelong one and will involve continued dedication to being compassionate with yourself as you face new connections and new levels of intimacy with the people you form attachment relationships with.

**Here are my wishes for you going forward:**

May you know the gift of trusting in your worthiness.

May you know the gift of great laughter and silliness.

May you know the gift of permission to feel. And the relief that comes when the pain subsides and makes way for peace again.

May you know the gift of feeling seen in all of your human truths and feel loved as a result.

May you know the gift of feeling heard and feel connected as a result.

May you know the gift of walking away from people who refuse to see or hear you and feel free as a result.

May you know the gift of solitude and trust that time alone does not mean disconnection.

May you know the gift of sharing your burdens with others and the truth that they feel honored.

May you know the healing of separating the past from the present.

May you know many, many secure connections where you experience true belonging and joy.

# Acknowledgments

I feel the urge to thank every single person who has ever been present with me, taught me to feel, and heal, and connect. There are so many of you and I have gratitude toward you all. If your name is not here, know that it IS written in my heart and story.

To my parents who worked so hard to give me so much more than you had. Mom, it was your brave cycle breaking that illuminated this path for me. And Dad, I know that you want my happiness and flourishing more than anything else on Earth.

To my incredible husband who walked through the dark with me, not knowing what would be on the other side, but somehow believing it would be beautiful. Your steady, kind presence keeps me feeling grounded and safe. And your ability to surrender to the creative and playful sides of life, keeps me from getting lost in all that is serious and deep. Also, you are not too bad on the eyes.

To my friends who helped raise me through the insecure years. You are truly magical people. The time and love you have poured out on me through so many seasons of life, but especially through my process of leaving an insecure attachment pattern and learning to love myself and others with freedom and fullness. Thank you, Megan, Carey, Dawn, Lacy, Piper, and Abby.

To all my siblings who continue to love me and sometimes listen to me, despite my incessant need to consider the ways that our childhoods affected us.

And to all the people who have cheerleaded me through this exciting and intimidating endeavor: Amanda and Jim, Whitney, Janelle, Chichi, Jill, Meg, Kaylyn, Callie, Rachel, Jessie, all of my PASS center loves, and the Denver Family Institute community. Your supportive spirit helped me write these pages.

# Delve Deeper

## RESOURCES

**Attachment Labs**
Classes and coaches specializing in attachment focused support.
AttachmentLabs.com

**Better Help**
A collective of virtual therapists who are available online and can be
accessed quickly.
BetterHelp.com

**National Domestic Violent Hotline**
Free, confidential support to help survivors of domestic abuse support
available 24/7 by calling 800-799-7223.
TheHotline.org

**PASS Center**
My therapy clinic in Denver, Colorado, where my team of therapists supports
individuals, couples, and families in deepening their attachment bonds.
PassCenter.com

**Psychology Today**
The largest online directory for finding therapists. You can search via topic,
treatment type, insurance, identity, and location.
PsychologyToday.com

**Suicide and Crisis Lifeline: 988**
Free, confidential support for suicide prevention, available by texting or
calling 988 anywhere in the United States.
988Lifeline.org

**Attachment Nerd**
Guides, workshops, and community support for anyone wanting to learn
secure patterns of relating with their children, partner, or closest friends.
AttachmentNerd.com

# SOURCES/BIBLIOGRAPHY

Ainsworth, Mary D. Salter, Mary C. Blehar, Everett Waters, and Sally N. Wall. *Patterns of Attachment: A Psychological Study of the Strange Situation.* London: Psychology Press, 1978.

Carlson, E. A. "A Prospective Longitudinal Study of Attachment Disorganization." *Child Development* 69 (1998): 1107–28.

Carrère, S., K. T. Buehlman, J. M. Gottman, J. A. Coan, and L. Ruckstuhl. "Predicting Marital Stability and Divorce in Newlywed couples." *Journal of Family Psychology* 14, no. 1 (2000): 42–58. https://doi.org/10.1037/0893-3200.14.1.42.

Cook, J., R. Tyson, J. White, R. Rushe, J. Gottman, and J. Murray. "Mathematics of Marital Conflict: Qualitative Dynamic Mathematical Modeling of Marital Interaction." *Journal of Family Psychology* 9, no. 2 (1995): 110–30. https://doi.org/10.1037/0893-3200.9.2.110.

Fonagy, Peter, Gyorgy Gergely, Elliot Jurist, and Mary Target. *Affect Regulation, Mentalization, and the Development of the Self.* New York: Other Press, 2002.

Gillath, Omri, Gery C. Karantzas, and R. Chris Fraley. *Adult Attachment: A Concise Introduction to Theory and Research.* Cambridge, MA: Academic Press, 2016.

Harlow, H. F. "The Nature of Love." *American Psychologist* 13, 12 (1958): 673–85. https://doi.org/10.1037/h0047884.

Hrdy, Sarah Blaffer. *Mother Nature: A History of Mothers, Infants and Natural Selection.* New York: Pantheon, 1999.

Karen, Robert. Becoming Attached: *Unfolding the Mystery of the Infant-Mother Bond and Its Impact on Later Life.* New York: Grand Central Publishing, 1994.

Levine, Amir, and Rachel S. F. Heller. *Attached: The New Science of Adult Attachment and How it Can Help You Find–and Keep—Love.* TarcherPerigee, 2010.

Lewis, T., F. Amini, and R. Lannon. *A General Theory of Love.* New York: Vintage, 2001.

Madhyastha, T. M., E. L. Hamaker, and J. M. Gottman. "Investigating Spousal Influence Using Moment-To-Moment Affect Data from Marital Conflict." *Journal of Family Psychology* 25, no. 2 (2011): 292–300. https://doi.org/10.1037/a0023028.

Shaver, P. R., and M. Mikulincer. "An Overview of Adult Attachment Theory." *Attachment Theory and Research in Clinical Work with Adults*, edited by J. H. Obegi and E. Berant, 17–45. New York: Guilford Press, 2009.

Sheinbaum, T., T. R. Kwapil, S. Ballespí, M. Mitjavila, C. A. Chun, P. J. Silvia, and N. Barrantes-Vidal. "Attachment Style Predicts Affect, Cognitive Appraisals, and Social Functioning in Daily Life." *Frontiers in Psychology*, 6, Article 296 (2015). https://doi.org/10.3389/fpsyg.2015.00296.

Siegel, Daniel J. *The Developing Mind: Toward a Neurobiology of Interpersonal Experience*. New York: Guilford Press, 1999.

Sroufe, L. A. "The Place of Attachment in Development." *Handbook of Attachment: Theory, Research, and Clinical Applications, 3rd edition*, pp. 997–1011. New York: Guilford Press, 2016.

Sroufe, L. A., B. Egeland, E. Carlson, and W. A. Collins. *The Development of the Person: The Minnesota Study of Risk and Adaptation from Birth to Adulthood*. New York: Guilford Press, 2005.

Stern, Jessie, and Rachel Samson. "Why We Treat Others as We Have Been Treated." *Psychology Today: The Heart and Science of Attachment*. www.psychologytoday.com.

Tawwab, Nedra Glover. *Set Boundaries, Find Peace*. New York: TarcherPerigee, 2021.

Tronick, E. *The Neurobehavioral and Social-Emotional Development of Infants and Children*. New York: W. W. Norton, 2007.

Wallin, D. J. *Attachment in Psychotherapy*. New York: Guilford Press, 2007.

# ABOUT THE AUTHOR

**ELI HARWOOD** is a licensed therapist who lives in Colorado with her husband, Trevor, and their three children. Eli has been nerding out on attachment research for the past two decades and is on a mission to help make the world a better place, one relationship at a time. She continues this mission in her clinical work, her writing, and running her mouth about attachment on social media. When she isn't working to make the world a more secure place, she is playing dress up with her kids, obsessing about her sourdough starter, and reminiscing about that one time that she won a set of globes as a *Price Is Right* contestant.

Visit her at AttachmentNerd.com or you can follow her on Instagram, TikTok, and Facebook @attachmentnerd.

Printed in China

SASQUATCH BOOKS with colophon is a registered trademark
of Penguin Random House LLC

28 27 26 25 24 23     9 8 7 6 5 4 3 2 1

Editor: Jill Saginario
Production editor: Peggy Gannon
Designer: Alison Keefe

Library of Congress Cataloging-in-Publication Data

Names: Harwood, Eli, author.
Title: Securely attached : transform your attachment patterns into loving,
  lasting romantic relationships / Eli Harwood.
Description: Seattle, WA : Sasquatch Books, [2024]
Identifiers: LCCN 2023006362 | ISBN 9781632174895 (paperback)
Subjects: LCSH: Attachment behavior. | Interpersonal relations.
Classification: LCC BF575.A86 H38 2024 | DDC 155.9/2–dc23/eng/20230221
LC record available at https://lccn.loc.gov/2023006362

ISBN: 978-1-63217-489-5

Sasquatch Books
1325 Fourth Avenue, Suite 1025
Seattle, WA 98101

SasquatchBooks.com

MIX
Paper | Supporting
responsible forestry
FSC® C008047
FSC
www.fsc.org